To: Fashad.
Thank you for your support.
Stay Blessed; Stay Encouraged
Stay Empowered
Stay pos it forward.
Yolanda Jones

LIFE GOES ON AFTER THE WAR

FROM UNIFORM TO CLASSROOM AND LIVING WITH PTSD AND OTHER SERVICE CONNECTED INJURIES; WHETHER MAJOR OR MINOR

YOLANDA JONES

The opinions expressed in this manuscript are solely the opinions of the author and do not represent the opinions or thoughts of the publisher. The author has represented and warranted full ownership and/or legal right to publish all the materials in this book.

Life Goes on after the War
From Uniform to Classroom and Living with PTSD and other Service Connected Injuries; Whether Major or Minor
All Rights Reserved.
Copyright © 2012 Yolanda Jones
v2.0

Cover Images © 2012 Yolanda Jones. All rights reserved - used with permission.

This book may not be reproduced, transmitted, or stored in whole or in part by any means, including graphic, electronic, or mechanical without the express written consent of the publisher except in the case of brief quotations embodied in critical articles and reviews.

Outskirts Press, Inc.
http://www.outskirtspress.com

ISBN: 978-1-4327-8943-5

Outskirts Press and the "OP" logo are trademarks belonging to Outskirts Press, Inc.

PRINTED IN THE UNITED STATES OF AMERICA

Acknowledgement

This book is dedicated to all my fellow Veterans who will be able to relate, to what it was like during the transitioning phase of returning home from Iraq and/or Afghanistan and having to readjust; trying to pick up from where we left off with our families, loved-ones and employments, prior to being deployed; as well as my day to day struggle of managing and living with PTSD and other service-connected injuries, be that major or minor.

Special Thanks to the Staff at the Temple VA for their ongoing Professionalism of Care and Services; to the Staff at the DAV- Waco Regional Office for their ongoing Support in Advocating for my Disability; to the Staff at the Comfort Suites in San Antonio when I just needed to get away and spend time alone; to the entire Gold Team Staff at the Dallas VA for making my Internship experience memorable and very rewarding as well as collaborating with the Bonham VA during my Internship; to my Veteran Colleagues and Coffee Buddies at the Dallas VA for sharing their Wisdom and Veteran experiences; to the Staff in Vocational Rehabilitation, TVC and DAV at the Dallas VA for always keeping me informed on employment prospects, education advancements and appeals.

To my Postal Deliverer from Westchester Postal Service who is also a Vietnam Veteran and always has a kind word to say each time he delivers my mail, and to the Woman employee at the Westchester Post Office whom without her knowing provided me mental and spiritual strength one day when I wasn't having a good morning, nevertheless her kind word energized me on that morning while I mailed my Manuscript for my first book "Scarred; but not broken." To the Secondary Postal Employee at the Main Post Office, I thank you for making my few visits to the main post office, pleasant and welcoming; to our family seamstress whom have been part of our family since my family relocated from New York about twenty-nine years ago, and has known me since I was in my mid-teens (Te Quiero Como una Madre).

Also, Special Thanks to the staff at Cash America Payday Advance for being very understanding, cooperative and empathetic regarding my financial situation and allowing me to set up a payment plan to pay off my loan; to the staff at Consumer Credit Counseling Service for assisting me with a payment plan and collaborating with many of my creditors, so that I was able to get caught up on my outstanding payments owed; to my former Co-Worker(s) who were invited to the celebration of my first book, I thank you for your ongoing loyalty.

Very Special thanks to an awesome woman and former Weekend-Supervisor; you deserve the Moon and the Stars. I thank you for showing what true leadership qualities should exemplify in a supervisor and on a management level. Let it be known, you did the best that you could, with what you had to work with. You will always rein the "Supervisor of the Year" in my heart.

Very Special Thanks to VFW - Unmet Needs, Soldiers Angels, Salute America Heroes, USA Cares and USA Together for all of their Emergency Assistance, during my financial hardship and transitioning. Without many of your support, as well as the support from my family I would have ended up like many Veterans who are not aware of these and other services available to them and are currently homeless, resulting in many living on the streets or in homeless shelters.

Very Special Thanks to my son and daughter for their unconditional love and support; to my mother and entire maternal family for their support in promoting my first book "Scarred, but not Broken." To my BFF of thirty-five years, who's a sister to me of whom people often cannot believe that we've been friends, and have stayed in contact for so many years; to my PR who is my right hand person, and has been with me from the beginning of my first book and isn't afraid, neither avoids controversial issues. Most importantly, my PR has been very dependable, someone whom I've been able to rely on to tell me what I need to hear and not what I want to hear; but from a very professional and logical perspective; to my significant other's family, for their unconditional support in allowing me to share a part of them. You know him as your son, your brother, your father. I know him as my Alpha Dog - My Lone Wolf - **He's My Anchor!**

Special Thanks to Blogtalkradio, "Victims Speak Out"; and to BBC [British Broadcasting Corporation] for their exposure and interest, in providing me a platform to voice and share about my experience during deployment in Iraq, and my decision to write and publish my first book, "Scarred, but not "Broken." I Thank You!

Finally and certainly not least, I want to thank God, for all my Blessings come from above!!

Preface

Although many Veterans discovered that picking up from where we left off prior to being deployed was not easy, neither was it reality; for many, our reality was that our families, loved-ones and places of employment had gone on without us. Nevertheless, they were not solely to blame, yet many of us were not ready to accept the reality, either. I know I sure wasn't. I couldn't accept that my daughter whom I left at fourteen years old and wearing braces and braids was now sixteen and wearing makeup and dating. I couldn't accept that my son whom was eighteen when I was deployed was now a young man at twenty and in college. I still wanted to be mother, yet I felt that I was robbed of my place and responsibility as being mother, because I was absent for almost two years of deployment and two years of their lives.

Yes, we have come a long way with the use of today's technology, with the invention of the DVR, so that the busy and working individuals' won't have to miss seeing their favorite shows. Then, there's the online accessible ways of capturing one's favorite daytime-afternoon and evening shows, also for the busy and working individuals'. However, life's precious moments are something that is not able to be played back on a DVR once gone; it can't be rewind. We can only rewrite in our minds of our vision of what our lives would've been like, "had it been played out this way or had it been played out that way." But the reality is, we weren't present to live in the moment with our family and loved-ones.

After the end of the deployment, the return from Iraq and my contract ended with the military (ETS), I felt a change in me both mentally and physically. I had a greater appreciation for family and just the "little things" that many in society tend to take for granted, i.e. water, as well as not allowing myself to sweat the small stuff. I also noticed that I had gained a few pounds; I'd gained eight pounds more. During my time released from the military I became indecisive as to what I wanted to do with the rest of my life. Although I previously obtained an undergraduate degree in Criminal Justice and had resigned from working for a Mental Health Agency in North Carolina, prior to being deployed, I was now in Grand Prairie, Texas and temporarily residing with my parents. The feeling was very overwhelming, because I had to start over as a single mom, age thirty-nine and no home of my own.

I wanted to return to the East Coast, but my previous place of employment had undergone a change to the Manage Health Care System; resulting in many of the mental health providers leaving the clinic to form their own private practices; in addition, my former supervisor had retired. Consequently, nothing was the same.

I eventually decided to remain in Texas and returned to school in pursuit of a degree in Counseling. I knew I no longer wanted to pursue a Law Degree, because I had a conscious; I could not see myself defending someone who was guilty, neither could I prosecute someone who I thought may be innocent.

Therefore, I enrolled in the first four year local college I knew, which resulted in it not being my best of choice. Soon after, I transferred to another University which later became another nightmare, in itself. Although I met some good colleagues as well as professors, there was one professor in particular whom I believe had it for me from the very beginning. This professor made my experience at this university a nightmare. Then, there were a group of Caucasian students whom always sat in the back of the classroom in one of my subjects; these students made my experience in this particular class very uncomfortable, for I heard them snicker and many times make fun of my northern accent and how I pronounced words that did not sound the same as a "Texan" dialect. But I knew, had I acted on my emotions, they would had been sorry, I would have caught a case and I would had been expelled from school; let alone placed in jail, more or less, in a psychiatric treatment facility. They weren't worth it.

Nevertheless, life has a funny way of placing the same people in my path, because one of the females that were in this click, we ended up being employed by the same employer; which I finally had an opportunity to confront her on a much more professional grounds.

During my transitioning, I've had the liberty of crossing the paths of many whom have been very helpful, genuine and very concerned about how Veterans are and have been treated. On the other hand, I've also crossed the paths of many who said that they respected and appreciated what Veterans have done for "our" country, yet these same people's actions have proven differently. There are many organizations promoting to help OIF/OEF Veterans and their families, but in actuality many of these organizations are a joke and have simply played the fiddle. I experienced firsthand what it was like, being employed by a particular agency, simply because I was an OIF Veteran. This organization's objective was to help OIF/OEF Veterans, however soon after I was hired this same employer changed from a Dr. Jekyll to a Mrs. Hyde. I began to receive constant verbal and emotional attacks by this employer who claimed to have a compassion for helping OIF/OEF Veterans. Ironically, I discovered later which it didn't take a rocket scientist to see that this compassion was geared towards only one branch of service who served in support of Operation Iraqi Freedom / Operation Enduring Freedom.

Finally, the ongoing services, treatments and disability appeals through the Veteran Administration Healthcare Systems continued to be a battle on civilian soil; the ongoing frustrations of incompetent medical staffs, resulting in many times pure disappointment, anger and resentment. Too often, Veterans have given up, either psychologically or physically because of constantly being denied of an injury or an illness, even though they may have supportive documentation, i.e. a LOD record of injury; which they have sustained during deployment and active duty status. Then, there are the Veterans who've given up on appealing for their disability simply because of the poor, distasteful and unprofessional attitudes they receive from many of the administrative staff at local Veteran Hospitals. I'm familiar with this experience, oh too well.

Living with PTSD as well as other injuries that I've sustained, whether major or minor have been a daily struggle for me. Although I'm able to identify and to avoid "when", "what" or "who" may be a negative trigger; managing my PTSD is and will continue to be a day to day challenge. This is my life, this is my story from uniform to classroom and living after the war with PTSD and other service connected injuries…

Information shared in this book is essential to telling my story; neither have I allowed the personal views or opinions of others to taint what I've expressed or experienced; for, it is my recollection of events that I've related them to and remember to the best of my knowledge.

Table of Contents

Chapter 1	**Road to Personal Recovery**............................1	
	Self-Assessment and Daily Maintenance 1	
Chapter 2	**Being Different**..4	
	A Distinguished Flavor 4	
Chapter 3	**Living with PTSD** 7	
Chapter 4	**Anxiety and PTSD** 10	
	Adjust and Compromised 10	
Chapter 5	**Scenarios** 13	
	Easily Triggered Responses; Not Easily Managed.....13	
Chapter 6	**PTSD**..17	
	The Perception of Being Misunderstood in the Civilian Workplace...17	
Chapter 7	**Therapy**...20	
	Building Trust and Rapport; Client - Therapist Relationship 20	
Chapter 8	**The Professor** 23	
	The "Click"; Trying to Exercise Self Control, to Avoid Catching a Case and Being Expelled from the Graduate Program 23	
Chapter 9	**Professor's Direction**..............................27	
Chapter 10	**Self-Awareness and Discernment**..........30	
	Disconnect from Classmates..................................30	

Chapter 11	The Oval Table and the Portfolio	33
	Being at Peace, but here's to "In Your Face"	33
Chapter 12	Graduation Day	35
	"I Yearned for This Day" Reflection on Life's Hardship and Overcoming Adversity	35
Chapter 13	Several Part-Time Jobs and Unfit Job Search	38
	Veteran Career Expos and Workshops	38
Chapter 14	Non-Profit	41
	Hired New Career; So I Thought	41
Chapter 15	Private Agency	48
	Abuse of Novice Management Power & Control Reliving Triggers	48
Chapter 16	Private Agency PART-II	52
	Hostile Work Environment; Triggers Continued Laid Off; the Best Thing That Could Have Happened & Bambooz'd; "Unfavorable for Hire"	52
Chapter 17	Therapist Relocated	63
	Reassigned Therapist (Psychologist); No Connection - No Rapport	63
Chapter 18	Resident VA Staff (Third Year Medical Residents)	66
	Veteran's Choice - Unprofessional VA Administrative Staff	66
Chapter 19	Struggling and Transitioning Home	69
	Local Non-Profit Charitable and Church Organizations & Available Resources for Veterans	69
Chapter 20	Memoir: Service Connected Injuries Appeals	73
	Appeal #1:	73
	Appeal #2:	74
	Appeal #3:	75

Chapter 21	Memoir 77
	DAV (Disabled American Veterans) There to Help Veterans; Starting Over Being Respected, Appreciated and Not Dismissed VES (Veterans Evaluation Services)..................................77
Chapter 22	Diagnosis 80
	Unsure (Misdiagnosis) Not being heard Masking the Underlying Problem; Instead, Being Prescribed Pain Medications 80
Chapter 23	False Alarm.. 83
	Statement Taken Out of Context 83
Chapter 24	Living with PTSD 88
	Living with PTSD and Other Service Connected Injuries Whether Major or Minor 88
Chapter 25	Recaps... 92
Chapter 26	Where Do I Go From Here?................................... 98

1
Road to Personal Recovery

Self-Assessment and Daily Maintenance

Since my return home and release from active duty status, I tried to pick up from where I left off prior to being deployed to Iraq, but it was difficult. Something was different. I was different and everything and everyone around me appeared different. I tried to shake this feeling and to believe that it was only in my mind, but it was real. I began to ask myself "where do I go from here?' I wanted so much to return to the East Coast and regain my position at the Mental Health Agency, where I was once employed, and prior to being uprooted and deployed. However, it was confirmed through a telephone call from a former co-worker that the clinic had gone under a major makeover and was now operating under the Manage Health Care System and many employees had resigned to sought employment elsewhere; many therapist had gone on to open their own practices and some accepted early retirement. In addition, my former supervisor was one who was no longer with the clinic and had retired.

Wow, I knew there was a possibility that this would happen, because prior to me leaving there were a lot of debate and mixed feelings about the Manage Care System taking over, which would affect the care and services of many mental health clients. The debates and discussion of concerns were always centered around how client's would be limited on how many sessions they would be allowed to see their Therapist; I guess it was wishful thinking, in only hoping that it wouldn't happen, but it did and now I was out of a job because at the time of my employment I was working as a Paraprofessional TANF (Temporary Assistance for Needed Families) Caseworker for the Mental Health Clinic. My role as a Paraprofessional TANF Caseworker was to conduct mental health screenings and random urinalysis as well as to collaborate with the client's Probation Officer, CPS Worker, the Court System, re: client's compliance with either the recommended or court mandated treatment(s).

Well, now I needed to adapt and adjust to making the best of a very uncomfortable situation; having to reside with my parents and residing in a state that I saw no future in; neither did I feel as though I belonged. Therefore, I proceeded to update my resume, attend job workshops for Veterans, and even presented on interviews. Still, something was missing and I wasn't happy. Ironically, although I had a terrible experience with the Unit that I was deployed with in Iraq, I still yearned for wanting to be back in the uniform. Was I crazy? Had I actually lost my mind; wanting to be back in the uniform that I once upon a time was not protected in? I felt lost and very confused.

Although I was home and on civilian soil, day in and day out it was difficult to drive on the roads. I felt myself becoming more irritated and easily agitated with other motorist who would either drive too slow or were driving too close to me.

I even began to have road rage and would become angry if someone cut me off in traffic; resulting in me thereafter following them and questioning "what the @$!% was their malfunction?" But of course they would stare at me nervously shaking and say, "I'm sorry."

There were times unbeknownst, that I would excel my speed beyond the speed limit, sometimes as high as 85-90mph; yet it never felt as though I was driving fast; instead it felt normal to me. However, my daughter at the time was sixteen years old who brought it to my attention that I was scaring her, because I was driving too fast. Nevertheless, my behavior resulted in my daughter not wanting to get into any vehicle with me, until I'd received psychiatric help; although I didn't understand what was happening to me, for I knew I didn't act this way prior to my deployment.

Had I lost my mind over in Iraq? More and more it was becoming difficult to drive and moreover I found myself driving around pot holes in the freeway and even on the local streets, as well as afraid to drive under the over paths. I became over hyper vigilant, in that I would carefully recon the over paths before driving under them.

I tried to cognitively recondition my thoughts, by telling myself that I was home and in a safe environment. But was I? Honestly, I didn't feel any safer on civilian soil than I did in Iraq; at least I knew my enemy were staring me in my face; however at home everyone I came in contact with whom I didn't know was my enemy; sadly, there are many days I still feel that way.

2

Being Different

A Distinguished Flavor

I tried to go on with my life, for I tried to put the Iraq and deployment experience behind me. I wanted to forget and I wanted to live a normal life without these strange feelings and impulsive behaviors that I was experiencing, but couldn't explain neither would my mind let me. What was even more difficult was that I had no-one that I trusted to confide in, without someone thinking that I was crazy or someone maybe wanting to have me committed to a psychiatric ward for being mentally unstable. It was apparent, that I was different and having been deployed and experiencing firsthand what racism was like, it was now again at my front door.

I believed that I was now, once again experiencing racism in the classroom. However, what was so devastating about this form of racism was that, I was experiencing it in a "Christian" University. Wow, how ironic was that. Well, being different I knew this feeling oh so well. It seemed as though being different had always shadowed me, as well as been my strongest trait.

About two months after my release from active duty status I enrolled in a local University, in pursuit of a Master's Degree in Counseling. My initial intention was to one day be able to become a Case Manager for Veterans, not so much a Counselor, nevertheless I was in for a huge awakening. Then again, it really didn't surprise me, if anything I was angry. Although I had awesome instructors for the first semester, prior to my voluntary transfer to another university, I can't really say that I have anything nice to say about the students or the administrative staff at this university. First of all, many of the students that attended this particular university appeared to have come from very affluent families; just based on over hearing many of their conversations.

Furthermore, few of the students were exchanged student whom were housed with many of these affluent student families in question, whom; of course, became accustomed to their lifestyles and behaviors; resulting in many of these exchange students disassociating themselves from individuals like myself whom were not born into an elite family or should I say born with a sapphire, ruby, emerald or platinum or gold spoon or a nanny to wipe our spoiled @#!. Of course many of these affluent students whom I'm referencing to were Caucasian and many of these exchanged students were either from small cities and villages from the third world countries...

As for the administrative staff, huh let's just say, since my parent's didn't play afternoon golf, break bread over afternoon tea with the elite wives and I didn't wear designer clothes, the administrative staff's attitudes and attention would had been better given to a one-legged lost dog than to me or any under-privileged student. Right about now, I'm sure you're going to say "so what, there's students and families who've attended this University and didn't receive the same mistreatment, because their son or daughter played sports or they, themselves participated in the University's great theology program. OK, well you just solved your own mystery....Now, go figure.

Too often it has been proven that many people preach the "Gospel", but few "Follow" the Gospel. Preaching and living how to treat your brother or sister of a different race or social economic status, speaks volumes.

If you're going to preach it, then you aught to apply it two-fold... I may be different, but I'm different with a distinguished flavor, one that is unique and with integrity; but more importantly, one that truly knows how to treat my sisters and brothers from a different ethnicity, regardless of his or her social economic background. Now, that's being a "True Christian."

This mistreatment from what suppose to be a "Christian" University", alone is enough to make any Veteran question their own belief and faith in Religion versus Spirituality.

3

Living with PTSD

Knowing and accepting the reality that I will always live with PTSD has been an ongoing day to day challenge for me. Since my return from Iraq I can't count how many times I dread getting out of my bed and having to report to my civilian job, due to the constant triggers that reminded me of the poor leadership which I was subjected to; let alone, ostracized, berated and tormented throughout my entire deployment. My ability to rationalize, along with my self-control, inner strength, as well as the intensive cognitive reconditioning of my thoughts; in order to refrain from falling back into that dark place, by acting on my emotions and keeping me from catching a case, continuously reminded me, "Yolanda, it isn't worth it?"

People say that they understand **PTSD**, but do they really? I don't believe many does. Honestly, I don't believe that many really **GET IT**. Many in society don't seem to grasp the extent or the magnitude of PTSD and how it can effect Veteran's cognitive perception of the world. Family, love-ones, friends, co-workers, all just doesn't seem to really get it. Sometimes Mental Health Professionals doesn't seem to get it, either. Many Mental Health Professionals expect for us Veterans to take a **"happy pill"** and go on with our lives without truly addressing our symptoms.

On the contrary to what some people may want to believe, **"getting over it"** isn't easy. A matter of fact, it isn't something that we can do. Furthermore, none of us want to live with PTSD, however we do have a choice to live, advocate for ourselves and to manage our symptoms in a proactive way. More importantly, many Veterans are choosing to not want to become dependent on medications that alter their thought process and cognitive functioning; therefore many prefer outside alternative therapeutic mental health treatments, opposed to what is currently being offered through the VA Healthcare Systems.

So I ask myself, why is it that this illness is so difficult for people to comprehend, embrace, treat and be sensitive to? What is **PTSD?** Consequently, based on all the information that I've gathered from my Therapists, Group Counselors, during my graduate studies, as well as from my own personal first-hand experience, PTSD is originated from an extreme or severely traumatic event, that causes recurrent of the events through nightmares, flashbacks, sounds and can even be triggered through a particular smell or taste.

For Veterans, many of our symptoms that will trigger a re-current event may be the sound of a helicopter, hyper vigilance, anniversary dates of traumas and losses, anger outburst or many times being provoked or an uncontrolled anger outburst, incompetent authority telling us what to do, irritability, easily agitation, hearing disturbing news, being easily startled, certain types of weather, sexual harassment, the smell of JP Fuel, disappointments, disloyalty, feeling threatened and yelled at, insomnia, seeing road kill, someone driving too close to us on the road or someone driving by us on the road too fast, hearing people speak in different languages especially in the language where we've been to war, also seeing people dressed in different clothing especially in the country that we've been during war, seeing people with certain facial features especially if the resemblance is from the country where we've served during war time, explosions, loud noises such as vehicles that back fires and fireworks during the 4th of July Holiday,

For me, hearing the sound of thunderstorms has been an ongoing trigger, for it reminds me of the sounds of the RPG's and Mortars. And, although it's been six years since my return from Iraq, I always feel safer at home and in my closet during the times of thunderstorms. My closet has been my safe place for the last six years, especially during inclement weather, involving powerful and raging thunderstorms.

Nevertheless, during this time I would stuff cotton balls and ear plugs in my ears. Thereafter, I would find solitude and place myself in a happy place within my mind and simply allow myself to be in the moment, with my mind body and soul, until the storms surpass. However, the daytime thunderstorms were different; instead, I'd turn on my stereo on high blast so that I could drown out the thunderstorms, along with placing the cotton balls and ear plugs in my ears, for added protection to prevent any damage to my ear drums from the high decibels.

However, it's most challenging and embarrassing to be out in public, to clinch and to not want anyone to notice that I'm experiencing a trigger from the thunderstorms. Well, that is what it's been like for me many times when I was at work, and all of a sudden the thunderstorms would occur. During this time, I would want to run into the company bathroom and hide and wait out the storm, but I couldn't; I had a job to do, so what could I do? Consequently, because of my job description; resulting in time restraints, I had to quickly apply cognitive reconditioning to my thoughts, and in doing this I quickly would tell myself that I was on civilian soil, and that what I was hearing was natural sounds; thereafter, I'd follow it through by calming myself down and exercising ten seconds of control breathing techniques.

4

Anxiety and PTSD

Adjust and Compromised

I have made many sacrifices and compromised my symptoms with family and loved-one, just to appease them all; without any of them actually knowing what I was truly experiencing, within the moment. Each time that I forced myself to be compromised, my palms would begin to sweat, I would get shortness of breath, light-headedness, stomach knotting and cramping, headaches and heart palpitations. But often times, they never knew. There were times few of them caught me holding my chest and trying to slow down my breathing, but they never associated it with "Anxiety"; No. Instead, like the general of society, they associated it with "Stress." They were not aware that I was in actuality experiencing a Panic Attack.

Nevertheless, many times my colleagues and loved-one couldn't understand why it was difficult for me to be able to walk into a local Wal-Mart or even the local Mall; considering that once upon a time, that wasn't a problem prior to me being deployed to Iraq. Thus, to avoid being the "dud" of the bunch and ruining everyone's evening I'd adjust and compromised my anxiety, by attending loud sporting events, amusement parks, and crowd. Even with family, it was very difficult for me to attend occasional family holiday dinners, although many times it was against my better judgment; which by the end of the evening I would be a total mess; resulting in me deciding to leave the event early.

Meaning, I had become irritable, easily agitated, and isolated. What was initially to be a fun filled day or evening would usually result in me regretting that had I remained home, my evening would've had a better and more positive outcome.

My Anxiety paralyzes me, for it keeps me from participating in the activities that I once enjoyed, it keeps me from adventuring into activities that I've always desired to explore and it isolates me from an opportunity of exposing myself for social networking.

I've been asked, what is it about the crowds, the loud sporting events, amusement parks, Wal-Mart, the Mall, or occasional family holiday dinners that causes the onset of my anxiety symptoms? Good question. I can only respond based on what I feel and that is, "fear of the unknown; the unexpected" whatever that may be.

Although I have tried taking baby steps, by presenting to the local Wal-Mart during the slower times of the day, it never fails nor seems to amaze me that there will always be customers who actually **"LIVE"** in the Wal-Mart stores, regardless of what time of the day I present, which I find to be outraciously ludicrous.

Ironically, I have spoken to many Veterans who feel the same, therefore I have come to a valid conclusion that Veterans with **PTSD and/or Anxiety** do not respond well when placed in a loud, closed-in and crowded place that compromises their inability to be cognizant of their environment, and to be able to react when needed.

Same is true for treating me to an afternoon matinee movie, or sitting alone for afternoon lunch at a table in a restaurant. To an average civilian person, this form of behavior is "not normal"; so, "they" say. However, to the average PTSD Veteran, like me this behavior is "very normal." And again, to family, friends and loved-one, they don't seem to understand, they don't seem to **"GET IT"** that many Veterans are "ok" with wanting quietness; I'm "OK" with quietness and sometimes I just want to be left in the moment with my thoughts.

Honestly, I believe much of the misconception that my family and loved-one have, which may have caused some slight disappointments is that, they expected or assumed that I would returned from Iraq and give me a few months, maybe a year or two and "she'll be back to her normal self." Yes, that was a misconception, because anyone who has been exposed to any form of war whether directly or indirectly is never the same and will never be the same, as they were, prior to being deployed.

On the contrary, there will always be a sound, a smell, a resemblance of some sought that will trigger a recurrent event of the trauma in which one has been exposed.

5

Scenarios

Easily Triggered Responses; Not Easily Managed
1. I recalled entering a local hardware store; in need of a air filter for my apartment, and although I searched high and low for what seemed like a good one hour for a particular filter; 14 x 18 x 1. I had no success. Therefore, as I was exiting the store, I decided to stop at the customer service counter, to inquire if the sales clerk could assist; by accessing their inventory computer system.

As I approached the counter, I noticed there were three sales clerks; however, one was assisting a customer, and the other was assisting the co-worker with the customer. Nevertheless, what caught my attention and agitation, to the fullest of all agitation was to notice the third sales clerk; leaning against the store's fax machine, while holding a stack of papers; meanwhile, she continued to avoid looking in my direction.

The more I made every attempt to call out for her assistance, the more she continued to ignore me; by looking off, as though she didn't hear me, nor see me. Wow, I said to myself...how lazy, asinine, and ridonkulus can some civilian people be? Yes, I'm aware I said ridonkulus and not ridiculous, because that is how my experience has been, interacting with many of the civilian customer service. Yet, I remained calm; but, I wanted so much to jump across the counter to slap this woman. But I knew, had I, I would've also caught a case.

Hence, about twenty minutes had passed; I then called out for assistance to the second sales clerk, when I noticed that he was through assisting the other co-worker and customer.

He asked politely, "Yes, how can I help you?" In short, I inquired about the air filter; at which, he was about to search the stores data base, until all of a sudden, I now became noticeable.

Yes, all of a sudden the previous mentioned, lazy, asinine, ridonkulus sales clerk wanted to assist, and wanted to appear as though she was so knowledgeable of the store's inventory. She stated, "14 x 18 x 1? No, we don't carry that size." Wow, and to think it actually had a brain and could articulate. Yes, she said a mouthful, so she thought; as a result, I became even more frustrated. I then told her in a very irritated tone, "That's all you had to say; had you assisted me, dumb@!#.

See, it's incidence (s) like that, which makes me and other Veterans regret getting out of bed, because of the fear that I will hurt someone; and, it's individuals like this sales clerk that causes a negative trigger, resulting in something that could've turned out to become fatal; given the circumstances of me being another Veteran with a shorter fuse.

2. Another trigger for me, which feels like a dagger in my spirit, is to be constantly criticized. It's one thing to have been berated, ridiculed, taunted, and ostracized by my commander during my deployment; which I also mentioned in my previous book, "Scarred, but not Broken", and it's another to be criticized and made fun of when I was a child in grade school; being made fun of because I was fat, and had dark circles around my eye; resulting in always being called porgy-pig and panda.

However, through the years and since I've transitioned and returned home, I've become more health conscious about what I eat, and how much I exercise. In addition, because I'm on certain medications, along with my diet and exercise, I've begun to drop more weight than I initially aimed for; although I never complained, because being in my forties, I enjoy the end result of wearing size six clothing again. More importantly, as long if I receive a clean bill of health, each time I visit with my primary care physician, that is what matters.

I know you're (reader) wondering where am I going with this? Well, because others around me have been either over weight-underweight or unhealthy themselves, it appeared that I've been the center of attention, to be criticized about my weight, comments such as...

"You keep loosing weight, you're going to blow away; Oh my God, where are you?; You're so skinny, you loose anymore weight you're going to look anorexic; Where's your booty?; Now you have a white girl's booty; You know if you keep loosing weight your breast are going to keep getting smaller."

OMG! Are they serious? Are they all serious? Do they have any idea what this is doing to me? Yet, every time I try to change the subject or redirect and focus the conversation on them and their weight and unhealthy lifestyle of diets, they always had excuses, whether it was gene problems, thyroid problems, medical problems, yada-yada-yada. I've heard it all. Yet, I was being criticized for loosing weight and wanting to be healthy.

With all of their criticism, they didn't know that I was battling my own fight with loosing my hair. Many times I was even questioned and criticized about my hair and how it looks as though it was getting shorter. I remember telling them that it was the medications that was making my hair fall out; but was it really? I still don't know for certain. What I do know is, when I'm alone and combing my hair I've cried many days, because of seeing chunks of my own hair falling into the sink; and I have no answers to why my hair is thinning and falling out; but I do know is, I'm being criticized and no-one seems to understand my battle that I'm fighting everyday, re: unexplained symptoms that I believe are caused from war related environmental exposure.

This alone has caused me many times to shut down, isolate, and become irritated, agitated, frustrated and very angry…

3. Although there are many triggers for me, I'm sharing a few of my true live, day to day triggers…another trigger for me is when last minute rules or instructions or plans are changed without giving me plenty of notice. OMG. Where do I even begin? Besides the loud noises, the mistreatment I received from my commander during my deployment, which still causes ongoing flashbacks for me, hence, sudden or last minute changes to my structured environment causes me to feel an increased level of frustration, anxiety, hyper vigilance, paranoia, agitation, irritation and helplessness.

Although I've made every attempt to explain and address this important concern to family members and loved-one, for some reason it appears that my concern has a very slow process of registering, or many of them just don't seem to understand the level and seriousness of my PTSD, and how my PTSD paralyzes my inner soul.

Consequently, there have been many times because of their failure to fully understand me and what I'm experiencing, that I shut them out, and isolate for days-weeks-even months. Nevertheless, the sad part of it all is, they don't know combat PTSD, because they don't **understand** combat PTSD. What's even worse is, because they **won't** take the time to explore and understand what combat PTSD is and its effects, therefore they can't help me, and they will never know me.

For, I am not who I was before deployment; I am someone whom they don't know, although I'm in the same body before deployment, my mind is not the same, and that is something they'll never comprehend, because they've never been to war!!!

6

PTSD

The Perception of Being Misunderstood in the Civilian Workplace

When I returned from Iraq, I noticed that there were many non-profit and private organizations looking to hire Veterans, while expressing their **"Patriotic"** duty to hire a Veteran. I was in awe how society appeared so concerned in welcoming the returning Iraqi Veterans. Nevertheless, several nonprofit organizations and programs were blooming like wild flowers and private companies were presenting at various career and Veteran Workshops everywhere, every week, every month. It seemed as though every weekend there was always a job fair being held and within that job fair was always some nonprofit or private organizations looking to hire a Veteran. However, the irony of these organizations was that, although they delivered an exquisite speech about how patriotic they and their company were and how they wanted to **"do the right thing in supporting our troops,"** their speeches were worth as much as the manure flown over crops for fertilizer.

There were and still are very few organizations that will go that extra mile to provide sincere and genuine services to Veterans and never ask the Veteran for a penny or even a dime. Then, there are organizations that in order for them to continue to be funded through grants or to continue to receive business loans to stay afloat, they have to prove on paper that a portion of their services are being offered and/or provided to Veterans. So, what do these organizations do? These sharks market the company, by using their foot puppets to lure in Veterans who are eager to obtain employment, and whether the hiring employer want to or not, in the back of their minds they're thinking that in order for their company or program to stay afloat they have to hire a Veteran; patriotic or not.

Consequently, I've had the opportunity to see what it was like to return and thereafter obtain employment within the civilian sector. Let's just say, it hasn't been easy, but very difficult to say the least; due to the civilian's perception of a War Veteran. For some reason, we are seen as **intimidating, aggressors, full of anger, abrasive, assertive, harsh, rough, insensitive, hostile and amongst some other vulgar means of expressions**, I'm sure. But, what I could never understand is that, for an example take two employees, one being a War Veteran and the other a plain Joe Blow; both having the same amount of time with the company, both at the same position and title. Moreover, the employer instructs a task for both to complete along with a dead line, however they both disagree with the deadline and doesn't believe that the deadline is a realistic deadline to accomplish. Therefore, both employees address their concerns by disputing the deadline date, using the same tone in their speech and without any threatening body gestures.

Yet, the majority of the time the Veteran is seen as more of a threat and more intimidating; which often results in the Veteran being reprimanded by a write up or terminated from his or her place of employment. Although this is not fair, it happens more often than society want to admit it. Why is it that? And, why aren't Veterans jobs protected in the Civilian Workplace, just like within Federal Work Place? Yet these same organizations say that they want to "support our troops."

I'd experienced firsthand how this felt. It was one thing to encounter a negative experience in Iraq, but it was another to be on civilian soil and to be employed by employers whom I always believed I had to walk on eggs shells in their presence. Furthermore, I believed as though I was always being watched by my employers, in hoping that I would, I guess…lose it…I don't know. But, for some reason it seemed that I was being watched like a hawk, as though I wasn't able to make any mistakes; same thing was true of my conversations were being closely monitored, in how I'd spoken to other co-workers. What the h…Trust me, if I wasn't angry prior to going into these workplaces, you can bet this was enough to perturb anyone and set the mood for the remaining of the day.

Too often I've been misunderstood, because I was a veteran and a woman of action and I believed in making the impossible, possible. While others wanted to sit around and wait until someone delegated to them what task to complete, by abusing and riding the clock, I'd on the other hand, would take the initiative and execute and worried about having to explain my actions later. Apparently, this **"take initiative"** attitude didn't play over well with the civilian sector. I'd also discovered that the management in the civilian sector was similar to the officer's in the military.

Many of them were about power and control, yet they lacked leadership qualities to truly motivate a staff on a positive level without intimidation and dictatorship. Nevertheless, although, I'd discovered that there are more kiss @!#, brown nosing and elbow rubbing in the private sector; it appears that there are always someone who wants to get to the top; no matter whose back they ride on to get there.

I was once schooled on how harsh the judicial system is on Veterans, which honestly choked me up. A very wised and professional person informed me that too often Veterans are sentenced with harsher penalties for homicidal crimes, due to the fact that we are known to be trained to kill. But should we? Why should we be punished for being trained to defend ourselves; especially when we are intentionally provoked and repeatedly harassed in the workplace, by the same people who hypocritically hires us, just because they want to get a response out of us and to confirm their theory that we're "unstable", because of our PTSD status. Yet, they hired us to be seen as "PATRIOTIC" and for the good of the company.

Now, who's really the **UNSTABLED** one?

7
Therapy

Building Trust and Rapport; Client - Therapist Relationship

She called my name, she was from India and she was my Therapist. We did not connect, for I had already judged her based on her nationality, instead of her qualifications. I was angry and meant her with total resistance. How could she help me? What does she know about what I've experienced in Iraq? After all, she's just like the rest of "them" that come over here to our country and take advantage of our educational system then mistreat us as though we're the second class citizens. What does she know about prejudice, racism, verbal and physical torture? Has she or anyone in her family experienced any of it; probably not. If anything, she probably came from the rich family in India.

During our first few sessions I just sat and I didn't want to talk; let alone engage with her. Nevertheless, she respected me and remained quiet as well; stated that she was going to leave it up to me, when I was ready to speak to her, even if it meant that we came to each session and just sat, which is exactly what we did. Wow, I could only imagine what was going through her mind. She had to of known how uncomfortable I was feeling and I'm sure she felt the same, but she remained professional, warm, empathetic and very genuine. Even after all that, I still wanted to be angry with her, but I couldn't. How could I?

After about the third or maybe the fourth session I fully opened up to her, at which I looked forward to every session, thereafter. For once, I didn't feel judged, but I felt heard; I had a voice again. She was someone I could trust and I didn't have to worry about feeling ostracized-berated or looked down upon. She listened and she provided me feedback, as well as provided alternative suggestions to help me manage my PTSD.

Every session was a task, as well as a challenge for me. It wasn't a normal client-therapist psychotherapy session, but it was more of a client-therapist psychoeducational focused session; whereby she employed a little bit of everything, i.e. Cognitive Behavioral Therapy, Solution Focused, Reality Therapy, some Adlerian. Very seldom was Carl Rogers applied, because it was always easy for me to express how I was feeling, therefore that was a no brainer, it was a given.

The more I attended my individual sessions the more I believed that I was going to overcome this illness, "PTSD", regardless of what the DSM-IV and other literature and research said about it and its recurrence. I wanted so much to be that example, that I'd soon ceased taking my PTSD medication and began putting in extra time volunteering at the local VA, and Co-Facilitating a WRAP (Wellness Recovery Action Planning) group, which I thought I was doing ok; after all, I was feeling ok.

Mentally and physically I was feeling strong. Consequently, I was practicing what I was facilitating, in that I was even applying my wellness maintenance to my daily recovery, as well. I never was one who believed in medications that controlled or altered one's mind, anyhow. Moreover, during this same time I was also employed fulltime job, while putting my daughter through college. Yes, I had a lot on my plate, but I still was determined to be that example and wanted to prove that Veterans could still live a normal life with PTSD.

Nevertheless, I was determined to be an example to all OIF/OEF(Operation Iraqi Freedom / Operation Enduring Freedom)

Veterans that "we" can beat this illness. Therefore, I became focused to set out to become that example. However, that focus later came with a heavy price that caused me to become too distracted and consumed that I didn't see it coming.

8

The Professor

The "Click"; Trying to Exercise Self Control, to Avoid Catching a Case and Being Expelled from the Graduate Program

I remember this day as though it was yesterday; this professor was known by many students and other professors as being very hard nose and sometimes even very ruthless. Even other professors seemed to fear this professor. A matter of fact, some didn't even care for her approach, same was true for many African American Students who didn't care for her and even believed that she may have been prejudice, at times. Hmm, I know I didn't care too much for her, especially after she placed me on a spot to ask me about my experience in Iraq and what I thought about it.

Yes, during one of the classes this professor inquired of my feedback on whether the news were correct on portraying what was going on over in Iraq and my response was, "No." I explained to her that the news only had shown what the Military Commanders wanted them to report, i.e. they will only allow patriotic soldiers to stand before the cameras to report that we were doing the right thing and how the soldiers were being taken care of, which were **ALL LIES!** Never have there been any soldiers asked to report to the public the truth of what was really going on in Iraq; instead, we were always kept from the cameras and news reporters. The real truth was that, many of our vehicles were not protected by armor; therefore, we were not protected. Hence, and at many times, we had to build our own armor for our vehicles, by using old parts from other vehicles and old metals from debris.

I never did share with her or the class about how the news failed to report that the military is still racially divided, neither had the news reported that many female soldiers had been raped by our own male soldiers. I could have even gone on and on about other unreported illegal events that occurred. Nevertheless, she thought I was going to confirm for her and the class about what her son had already reported to her, about how much we were doing such a good job over in Iraq, but I didn't want to bust her bubble. Neither, did I want to relive anything; I just wanted to move forward with my life and start anew.

From the duration of the time that I was in this graduate program, as well as having her as my instructor, it was a nightmare. To this day, I don't believe that she was fair with my final grade. Nevertheless, from that point on, other professors as well as a former advisor had suggested that I avoid taking any courses under this professor; which by the Grace of God I did. However, I will always believe that the final grade she administered for record was intentional; considering I transferred into this university with a high GPA track record.

Although, what is done is done; the important thing is, I graduated and I never have to see this professor ever again and she may have taken away my joy, just for that moment, but my degree was something neither she, nor anyone will ever take away from me.

Then, there was the incident in another class which involved a "click" of Caucasian females. These students sat in the back of the classroom of one of my subjects, and were always heard making fun, snickering and talking negatively about other classmates which disturbed me and made my blood boil; but when it happened to me, it triggered a negative response within me.

These students enjoyed sitting in the back of the classroom; they also made my experience in this particular class very uncomfortable, for I heard them snicker and many times made fun of my northern accent and how I pronounced words that didn't sound the same as a "Texan" dialect. But I knew, had I acted on my emotions they would had been sorry, I would've caught a case and I would had been expelled from school; let alone placed in jail or in a psychiatric treatment facility, because the end result wouldn't had been pretty. So, I had to re-evaluate myself, my age, where I was, my purpose for being in the graduate program and where I wanted to go in life, which was to utilize my degree to help other Veterans. Therefore, I then told myself, "They weren't worth it, or my energy."

Although I endured the endless agony of continuously attending class and trying to place my mind in a happy place, by blocking these ignoramus individuals out of sight out of mind, it was not easy to do; nevertheless I saw this experience and my patience as a test and a daily challenge. I began to see them as my enemy, they were in this click and honestly I believed them to have been prejudice in their own subtle way; just by their stares, and subtle prejudice remarks or statements when the classroom topics of discussions were about race.

Overall, I didn't care for them. Yet, I struggled daily of wanting to confront them, but I knew I had to exercise self-control and tell myself that they weren't Iraqis, but simple, ignorant, close-minded, sheltered, self-absorbed individuals, who I felt very sorry for their future clients, whom they were going to service, one day.

I remember their faces, I remember the clothes they always wore and I remember what they always brought to class to eat. I remember them and the incident so well that it has stuck with me, for so long until a year later when I meant up with the one in particular. Nevertheless, life has a funny way of placing the same people in one's path, because one of the females that were in this click we ended up being employed by the same employer, and once again a similar incident, involving me and this individual, once again occurred. Yes, she was the main one of the click then, and it was apparent that, even after grad school, her behavior had not changed.

Consequently, she was still making fun of how people were pronouncing their words or incorrectly using a word and that someone happened to, once again be me. But this time, she had me all twisted.

Having PTSD has been a daily battle and challenge for me to contain; whereby keeping my composure in tact; especially when the trigger is so strong, and forever reminding me of the recurrent traumas that I'd been subjected to, during my experienced in Iraq; under the poor leadership [the ridicule, the taunting; berating, gallivanting, racial discrimination, etc., etc.].

Nevertheless, after I addressed my concerns to her that I didn't appreciate her making fun of how I spoke and neither did I appreciate her doing the same thing when we were in graduate school, she tried to act as though she had amnesia, by stating that she didn't remember us being in the same class; although I refreshed her memory.

Thereafter, I continued to speak to her woman to woman, professional to professional by how it's about time that she grew up and behaved as an adult and not behave as though she was still in high school, by correcting people. Of course she wasn't ready to hear the truth, because she quickly became defensive, slammed down her headphone and stormed out of the office. I was now ready to move forward in placing this chapter behind me in my life…

Although this co-worker was a "negative trigger" for me; as a Veteran, one who've been subjected to much criticism, by this co-worker, I believe that given light of the circumstances, I conducted myself very well…Lord knows, it took a lot of cognitive reconditioning of my mind.

Had I been any other Veteran with a shorter fuse, the outcome would've been tragic.

9
Professor's Direction

I remember experiencing some financial hardship, in that I was only working partime which wasn't enough to pay my basic household bills, other outstanding bills prior to deployment, as well as paying for the continuous major mechanical repairs on my vehicle. Then, my mother took ill; thereafter multiple family members took ill. So much was happening all at once, that it became so overwhelming for me to digest; along with trying to manage my own health regarding my recurrent flashbacks of the sounds of the RPG and Mortars. I began to ask myself, what am I doing? Who am I kidding myself to think that I can distract myself, by pursuing an education?

Feeling overburdened and overwhelmed I went to my professor, yes the one that I already had a tenuous relationship with to address my concerns of possibly being allowed to miss a day or two of class, so that I could take care of my personal business, and so that it wouldn't affect my grades or studies. Well, so much for my honesty and trying to be truthful, because her response was pure sarcasm; in that she suggested "Maybe this isn't for you." Instead of her being empathic and understanding of my situation and exploring alternative options that could help me to be successful during my graduate studies, this is what she tells me. Just for that moment I was stiffened with anger, disappointed and appalled that a professor could be so cold and constricted.

There was another incident involving this professor and a group project. I was assigned to a group, I believe it was six of us and each set of two had to work on a specific outline. Well, in short because I was a Sergeant in the military I knew how to delegate and not feel as though I had to take the credit for any completed task. Therefore, I compiled **ALL** the information. Yes, did you read correctly? **ALL** the information I compiled, and I designated my partner to be the presenter to explain the material, which she and I had prior agreed to do so; as well as what the professor had instructed that one of us did. Well, this instructor called herself placing me on the spot, by questioning, "So Yolanda what did you do?" When I explained to her that I was the one who compiled the material, she confronted me in front of the class, by saying that she could not believe that I compiled the material since I was not the one who presented it. Wow! I was very insulted and humiliated. As an end result, I received a very low final grade and my partner received the grade that I should have received.

Now, I know you're asking why I didn't fight it. Why should I? What good would it have done? Here, I was a **"defected"** African American Veteran with PTSD; unemployed and a single mother. She was a well-known Caucasian Professor, well known in the community with tenure. **WHO WOULD HAVE LISTENED!!!!!!!!!!!**

I later discovered that this professor had her selective picks of students and ironically her selective chosen were the same students who were the previous mentioned that were in many of my subject classes. How ironic was that? I soon began to look back at where I was in Iraq and how I saw my experience there as being Hell, then I began to realize no matter where I go Hell is everywhere and it can't be avoided, but faced head on. I soon began seeing this professor and experience similar to the trauma I encountered with the "Untouchables" in Iraq (The Commander, First Sergeant, S-1's, Co-Commanders and SFC).

I later sought direction from other professors, who provided me with suggestions and guidance which it resulted in becoming very helpful. Their guidance also lessened much of my anxiety; in that

I was able to vent my frustration of how I was feeling towards this professor.

Again, I was continuously being instructed to avoid taking any courses under this professor. A later discovery surfaced, in that prior to my former advisor retiring, I learned that this professor had predestined me to fail. I was shocked to have learned this revelation, and to know that she was hoping for me to **drop from the program**. OMG! I couldn't believe that I was hearing this from another professor. How could, or why would a professor predestine a student to fail, simply because she doesn't like them; or because the student(s) doesn't agree with her political views regarding the war in Iraq. OMG! You have got to be kidding me. Wow, that was a shocker.

Anyway, during many of my conversations with the latter of my professors, many of them provided me with positive feedback on what I could do to avoid feeling frustrated and angry, as well as improving myself through self-awareness, as a future clinician. Nevertheless, through their guidance I had also learned that, there will always be individuals, sometimes even professors who may not like a student or even want to see a student excel or become successful, and many times it may not be anything that the student may have done, but it may simply be the professors way of projecting what is really going on in their own lives onto that student. This, in and of itself was enough for me to hold onto, in order to get me through to graduation day. So I thought.

10

Self-Awareness and Discernment

Disconnect from Classmates

Attending graduate school was quite difficult, to say the least. For, there were many times I wanted to quit and it wasn't because I couldn't execute the work or projects, but it was due to the fact that I'd become more aware of myself and disconnected from the classmates. I'd also learned that many of my classmates had come from high social economic status, which it had showed in their attitudes and the crowds they associated with. Nevertheless, this environment made it more clear to me why our society is the way that it is, with regards to ignorance, segregation and racism. Yes, I said it right **SEGREGATION**. We are still more segregated than many of us want to own up and believe; as a result, this caused me to disconnect from my classmates whom I discerned as not being truly genuine, but very fake in their approaches towards me.

Remininicing during the time I spent in Iraq, I can truly say that there were some Iraqis whom I felt their genuineness of wanting "us", the military there to protect them; they appreciated our presence; they saw us as their safety net, and I saw it in their eyes; I felt it in their touch when they reached out to try to grab at us when we walked through their cities and markets. Not here. Sadly, I felt more accepted by some of the Iraqis than I did from my own class mates. Why is it that although we may be at war with other countries, yet many good people within that same country treated many of us soldiers better than our own that we attend school with, work with, live next door to or even attend church with?

Prior to being deployed to Iraq I didn't care about anyone but myself; as long if "Yolanda" got hers; I didn't care if anyone else got theirs. My motto before being deployed was, "this is a doggy-dog world, so you have to get yours, before you get got." However, the deployment in Iraq had changed me. I was not the same. I'd gained a new perspective and love for life and for people. I no longer was selfish, self-absorbed or self-righteous. Although I had now gained a zero tolerance for stupidity and bull @#!%, I'd returned home with good intentions of wanting to continue to better myself and to make a difference in society, by being part of something greater than myself.

As I continued to press forward and attend classes, I noticed how I became more and more withdrawn from many of my classmates, for many of them were so transparent to me. Their smiles became so incongruent with what they were saying and what I truly felt in my core and it wasn't at all sincere. But, how could I've expressed this feeling to my advisor or professors without them thinking that I was being paranoid or if it had anything to do with my PTSD? That was the problem, for I couldn't share these feelings of how I felt about my classmates to the faculty; therefore I kept it to myself, which was obvious because it manifested itself through other ways, through total isolation and by me shutting down.

Soon after, negative attentions were drawn to me by students who I witnessed snickering amongst themselves, while passing me in the halls or I'd noticed they would avoid sitting next to me in the classrooms. Once again, I felt alone. And once again, it was the similar experience I felt in Iraq when the Commander of my Unit who ordered many of the soldiers not to associate with me, because I initiated an internal investigation throughout the Unit, due to advocating for a female soldier; by reporting a criminal incident against a male

Platoon SFC. Yes, I was now being triggered and having to relive a very uncomfortable event.

Day after day, week after week, month after month, semester after semester seemed like eternity. In actuality, I was just trying to survive; yet, trying to keep myself in the present...while all along, no-one ever knew what I was experiencing; then again, no-one ever genuinely reached out to inquire.

11

The Oval Table and the Portfolio

Being at Peace, but here's to "In Your Face"

Although I looked forward to this day, I was also confident, for I knew I had worked very hard and diligent to present my portfolio. As we were separated in groups and instructed to wait in the halls until our groups were called, I observed the facial nervousness of many of the students that surrounded me. The air was amidst with tension, yet and for once I was at peace with the universe; mind, body and soul. One would describe my feeling as, momentarily peaceful. This was it; this was my time to prove to **that one** professor, to all my classmates, but more importantly to myself, that once a soldier always a soldier and failure is **NEVER** an **OPTION**, regardless of the circumstances!!!!

Our group was then called, "Next Group!" at which we all took our seats around the oval table. The aura of the room was that of a panel discussion. As I entered the room, I observed all the portfolios were aligned across the table, and I noticed that my portfolio was the largest and well defined out of them all. Looking at my portfolio, one could tell that much precision and hard work was put into it. Therefore, it wasn't difficult at all to single out which portfolio belonged to me.

Each professor asked a question and each student took turns to respond. However, what was so interesting about this event was that each time a professor asked a question I waited to give my classmates a chance to respond, hence each time an opportunity presented itself for me to interject, and I did. Nevertheless, I articulated well and without any hesitation, which caused many stares and mouths to drop in awe because this was the first time throughout the entire program that I participated and articulated as well as I did and with such confidence. I'm sure they all were wondering what had happened to "Yolanda", as though I had been mechanically rebuilt [smile]. But, nothing was wrong, let's just say this was my way of saying, **"In Your Face" to** all those whom thought I was beneath them.

Throughout the entire graduate program I believed many of the students saw me how I saw myself, at that time; a **defected** Veteran with PTSD. However, similar to the attitude of that particular professor, I believe many of the students took on the same attitude as she did, in believing that I was not capable or had the potentials to complete the program, just because of my PTSD. Many times it was so obvious in their demeanor that they never had to say a word, which caused me to discern and disconnect from them.

Anyhow, after all questions were completed by the professors, they announced that everyone in the room had passed. Although many were anxious to hear the announcement, I on the other hand was just happy of knowing that I had survived the worst and the worst was the professor, who predestined that I would fail the graduate program. Hence, it was more of a victorious moment for me to have conquered and defeated when all **odds were against me**. Nevertheless, I walked away without saying a word to anyone, for I knew nothing was definite because within a nano of a second anything could've changed and mishaps such as unknown discrepancies could've happened. Yet, I still trusted no-one, especially based on my past military experience, of being too familiar with the unknown happening and documents, all of sudden disappearing.

Yes, I knew things like that could actually happen and no-one would ever have a clue…so they would say. I also knew that graduation day was slowly approaching and much still had to be accomplished. Therefore, I remained humble…

12

Graduation Day

"I Yearned for This Day" Reflection on Life's Hardship and Overcoming Adversity

The day was finally here and all my family and loved-one were present, except my mother whom was at home ill. However, although I yearned for this day and I was adorned in my graduation cap and robe, I still was experiencing mixed emotions. On one hand, I was happy that I no longer had to return to class or to see that particular professor, or to read anymore text books, unless I decided that I wanted to pursue my Ph.D., which I didn't. On the other hand, the moment didn't feel real, for it seemed as though I was experiencing one of my dreams within a dream.

Yet, at the same time I was experiencing sought of like an outer body moment of seeing myself going through the motions of the graduation. Furthermore, I was experiencing multiple physical pains, i.e. an excruciating headache and throbbing and shooting pain in my wrist due to a service connected wrist injury. Nevertheless, for this to be an exciting moment and event, much of it was too overwhelming to digest all at once.

The gymnasium was packed and very noisy with many of the graduation party's family and friends who traveled near and far, and everyone in the graduation class were as happy for this moment, as I. Although I was happy that this moment was finally here, I was also experiencing an increased level of anxiety. All of a sudden I felt a sense of endless agony; hence, my palms began sweating and my heart began racing and for no reason at all, I soon became very irritated and easily agitated each time a family member or my loved one asked me a question. At that moment, I knew that this event couldn't be over fast enough.

Moreover, I just wanted to turn around, get in the car, drive home and crawl back in my bed and pull the covers over my head and stay there for the remaining of the day. Furthermore, I didn't want to go out and celebrate with the family after the ceremony nor did I really want to take any pictures. Physically I was present, but psychologically I didn't feel totally present and in the moment. However, for the sake of my family, and loved-one and for their graciousness and willingness to attend the ceremony, to celebrate on the special occasion, I allowed myself to place my mind in a happy place in order to get through the event. As a result, I survived and was glad that it was finally over.

As I began to reminisce on the road in which I traveled to arrive to this day, I couldn't help but reflect on life's hardship and how I overcame many adversities. Nevertheless, what has helped me to never waver in my decisions and to stand strong whenever those in authoritative and dictatorship positions tried to knock me down [literally speaking] was that I'd adopted a motto for myself to, "look at every opportunity as a challenge and face every adversity as a path for growth."

Advancing in my education has been an ultimate goal of mine; although my desired area of interest has always altered, depending on life's circumstances. Yet, I never wavered in my quest to pursue nor obtain a higher education, in spite of the many hurdles and obstacles that lied in my path. Many have sought for me to fail. Apparently, no matter how hard they all tried, it was never in the original plans for my destiny. But, they tried.

I recall on the morning while I was getting ready for this day, I remember my daughter telling me that she didn't remember seeing me ever not attending school. I smiled because as a mother that was great to hear. I'd rather that she said that, than to say that she's always saw me in a club…Well, the reason my daughter said that she didn't remember seeing me ever not attending school was because, I'd always been enrolled in some local college, regardless of what personal circumstances I was going through. Yes, from the time my children were born, until they were young adults in their early twenties, I've been enrolled in college; trying to better myself as a single mom; trying to avoid the single mom myth and statistics.

Although I've been married, divorced and even dated and been a single mom many times in between, nevertheless, I've never wanted to be labeled a single mom statistic which society believes that children raised in a single parent home usually end up as high school drop outs, teen pregnancy, on drugs, or committing crimes or into gangs. No, I didn't want that label or stigma for myself or for my children. Furthermore, I wanted my young adult children to one day be able to look back on my graduation day and be proud of their mother's accomplishments, in spite of all the hell I've been through; knowing that I never folded, but I finished what I started, even though all adversities that stood before me.

Consequently, some people say they have three strikes against then in society, which is the reason they believe that they have such difficulty with advancement at their place of employment or receiving fair treatment at school, etc., etc…Well, let's just say, I stopped counting a long time ago; because I've learned no matter where I go, someone is going to feel intimidated or infuriated by what I've accomplished in life. More or less, we live in a competitive society; people are so consumed in competing and advancing one another, instead of competing and improving oneself…

13

Several Part-Time Jobs and Unfit Job Search

Veteran Career Expos and Workshops

After returning home and after weighing all my options of re-enlisting, I was informed that had I re-enlisted my next deployment would've been to Afghanistan, and that I would've been deployed with my own Unit. Wow, the offer sounded very appealing; however the catch was that the military couldn't guarantee that I wouldn't leave before my daughter's high school graduation, May 2007; and, considering that I'd previously missed my son's high school graduation while serving a tour in Iraq, I wasn't about to risk another mother's only moment of opportunity. Therefore, I completed the remaining of my military contract obligation and ended my military career, forever in 2005.

Since I decided to remain in Texas, I enrolled through the Workforce Center, thereafter began searching for employment, as well as attending various Veteran Career Expos and Workshops, which I didn't find many of the Expos and Workshops helpful. It seemed as though many of these Veteran Career Expos and Workshops were more interested in, and considering younger soldiers in their late twenties to mid to late thirties, or soldiers with more years of active duty service. Moreover, many of these organizations were hiring for Police Officers, Detention and Correction Officers, Dart Operators, Construction Workers, Warehouse Forklift Drivers and other Heavy Machinery Operators. Hence, the problem with many of these positions was that there was also an age cut off.

As for the Forklift Driver, one had to show proof of an active forklift license, whether it was a military or civilian license. Consequently, during my years in service I was certified to drive a 4, 000 and a 20,000 ton hydraulic forklift, due to my primary MOS- Automatic Logistics, which was needed due to having worked in a Class IX Warehouse or in the Motor Pool Section. However, because I didn't have an updated or active forklift license, I wasn't able to apply for any forklift warehouse positions.

In addition, I didn't see many clerical or secretarial positions being offered and if so, they were being offered through a staffing company; opposed to the direct hiring company. Besides, due to my service connected wrist injury, I was in too much pain and didn't see how I would acquire obtaining a clerical position with any private company, other than obtaining a clerical position through a Federal Agency, while wearing a wrist brace. Therefore, I didn't foresee a civilian company accommodating me with a specialized keyboard, if I were to be hired at that time.

Of course there were many stations set up for individuals inquiring about enrolling into various local and online courses. However, none of the colleges caught my interest. After attending about two maybe three Veteran Career Expos and not being totally satisfied with the outcome, I decided it wasn't worth attending any future workshops.

On a brighter and more positive aspect, the Veteran Career Expos and Workshops is an awesome way for Veterans to come together to network; especially if Veterans have lost contact with a battle-buddy, or even if a Veteran just wanted to be amongst other Veterans, just for a day. The Veteran Career Expos and Workshop is also a great way to meet new comrades whom can relate to some, if not all of the experiences that only another Veteran can understand and relate to.

As a Veteran, you know you're amongst family when you walk

through those doors; it's a certain aura in the air; no sweaty palms, no racing heart, no sense of irritation or aggravation, no loud noises, no feeling of wanting to rush home, everyone is warm, genuine and concerned. It's a feeling that only Veteran to Veteran can comprehend.

There were many other programs available to transitioning soldiers, seeking employment; so many that I can't recall the names off hand; however I know for certain that I've made a least one or two attempts which didn't pan out too well, thereafter, I simply became irritated, disappointed, and refused any further of their services. I decided then to seek employment search on my own.

Since my return and transition from Iraq, it has been very difficult for me to obtain and maintain steady employment. I've held several part-time positions, just to make ends meet in order to pay my basic bills and put my daughter through college. Nevertheless, due to bull@#!$ policy and procedures from nonprofit and private agencies, which I refused to lower my standards or compromise my integrity, it has either resulted in me quitting many of my part-time jobs or the employers finding me to be unfit to continue in the positions.

I've learned that there are two types of people in the business world, regardless of the field or the line of work; **1. Those who are compassionate at what they do and the people they serve and 2. Those who are self-centered, self-absorbed and just don't give a @#!$.**

Well, for some reason I seem to continue to end up being employed with the latter; those people who are self-centered, self-absorbed and just don't give a @!#$, which triggers a recurrent flashback of my experience in Iraq. No matter what I do or not do; or even avoid, something seems to trigger a recurrence of events in Iraq, which has a lasting and daily effect on how I manage and/or resolve situations with civilian employers…

14

Non-Profit

Hired New Career; So I Thought

It was January, 2009, and this was supposed to have been a very special job for me, so I thought. Nevertheless, it was a day for me to finally make a difference and to be part of something bigger than myself, for I would be helping my fellow Operation Iraqi and Enduring Freedom Veterans. I guess I went into this expecting too much and certainly something different from all the rest; at least that's what I wanted to believe.

Throughout my life I've meant many people of diverse cultural, religious and spiritual backgrounds and I've experienced many major close to death situations. However, as a child growing up and attending Sunday school and learning about the evils in the bible such as the Garden of Eden and all the trickery's of the Serpent, or how evil comes as a thief in the night, or how evil comes in sheep's clothing or even how once upon a time evil was the most beautiful angel in heaven until the Lord cast him out. Well, I knew that evil wore many faces, but I never knew hell had so many doors, because I walked right through it…

On March, 19, 2009, while at work one morning, I was introduced by an in-house agency email, by my supervisor; acknowledging my educational and background experience. Moreover, it outlined my job description, in that I'd conduct intake psychosocial assessments and I'd develop some peer support groups, since I was at that time, already a certified WRAP (Wellness Recovery Action Planning) facilitator. In addition, many of the vendors were also advised should they have any write-ups to report about their practices, that I'd be the contact person to forward the information to, which then, I'd update the information to their vendor's book. More importantly, it was conveyed that my position would allow more free time for my supervisor to conduct program management, community education, marketing and trainings. So I thought.

At the start of my employment my relationship with my supervisor was one that appeared to be very open and genuine. For, I would accompany her on several community outreach meetings, which resulted in people being interested in me as a Veteran and wanting to hear about my experiences over Iraq and depending on their level of sincerity of wanting to know, as well as me being cognizant of the environment in which I was sharing such information, many times I had no problem sharing my experience to anyone who wanted to listen. After all, I'd been home for about four years at that time, and had been in ongoing therapy, which had taught me that the more I talked about my experience, the more I would be able to better manage my PTSD and move on.

Well, after a while this attention did not go over too well with my supervisor, because soon after, her attitude and entire disposition towards me began to change in such a very negative light; in that I was no longer allowed to accompany her on any future meetings, nor was I to speak at any engagements without her prior critique of what I was going to speak about. I had now become confused as to the reason I was hired. I began to question myself, was she jealous of me because I was a Veteran?

I couldn't understand what was happening or why my supervisor's sudden mood change, but whatever her reason was, all of a sudden she had to approve what I was and weren't to say, especially when the topic involved my experience in Iraq to the predeployment soldiers who were preparing to be deployed; even though there were times many of them inquired and wanted honest feedback and first-hand knowledge from someone whom actually been over to

Iraq; opposed to looking at a power point slide by someone who never even wore a uniform.

Yet, she rather that I showed the soldiers a power point slide that was, in my opinion too graphic, illustrating pure death in Iraq that she compiled through various "marine" soldiers, so she said. As a result, I refused to show the graphic slides, for this was a trigger for me and she knew it. Nevertheless, she didn't care; instead she yelled, and screamed at me, as well as continued to say that I was being insubordinate for not following a direct order. The entire time, while she was yelling at me, I temporarily began slipping back into that dark place; all I saw were her lips moving; I no longer heard what she was actually saying, because for a brief moment I had blocked out the remaining of what she was saying.

Yes, I had a temporary flashback of when I was in Iraq. I remember a similar incident of when I was called in twice; once to stand before my First Sergeant and Commander, while they toyed and gallivant in my face and the second was when I was signaled to report to the Commander's and S-1 tent, while I was berated by many of the high ranking officials.

This woman wasn't stupid; she knew exactly what she was doing. Again, she didn't care and I believe to this day, she wanted to spark a negative response from me; just to be able to say that because I was a returning OIF (Operation Iraqi Freedom Veteran) that I was mentally unstable. But, I really wasn't the unstable one; although she was beginning to just trigger a negative response within me.

As days and weeks had progressed, our professional relationship became even more tenuous and day by day she became more emotionally and verbally abusive towards me, to the point that she would call me in her office, then would yell and accuse me for following instructions that she directed me to do, then try to back pedal by instructing me to call the vendor and explain to the vendor that "I" misunderstood what she was wanting. For an example, my supervisor kept mentioning that she wanted to host a homecoming event for the Marines and their families, which she provided a list of suggestions, stating that we still needed a speaker. According to her, the list she provided, the speaker had to be someone who had to be either a "politician, actor, etc.; that person would be used to thank the Marines for their services.

Well, in my quest to locate someone who would be appropriate for this event, I spoke to my supervisor to propose to use a particular person who not only was a former Marine, but at that time was currently very well-known and were doing great things within the community.

My supervisor's response was, yes, that would be great if she's available." Therefore, after I contacted this particular person and explained to her the purpose of the event, she was honored and accepted the invite and I was happy. But it didn't last long, because after I returned to inform my supervisor that the speaker had accepted the invite, my supervisor bluntly said, "No, she's not going to work." I stood surprised and shocked. Was she serious? Now, I had already prior consulted with my supervisor about this person as well as this person's credentials, therefore it wasn't like my supervisor didn't know anything about this person. But for her to be that ruthless and insensitive and bluntly say, "No", after this woman had already accepted the invite, it was unacceptable in my eyes.

I then asked my supervisor, Why, I thought you said it was a go, for me to go ahead and ask her if she would be available to be our speaker. My supervisor then stated, "We wanted someone who was more of a celebrity, like a professional athlete; just tell her that you misunderstood." What? My rebuttal was, but I didn't misunderstand, I know exactly what you said. My supervisor's response was, "but she doesn't have to know that."

OMG! If this woman was not sitting in front of me saying this and breathing, I wouldn't believe that she actually had a heart that was pumping. How could anyone be this cold and callous? As a result, I had to email this speaker and explain to her that there was a miscommunication and that I've been instructed that for this event a celebrity was more preferred.

Of course, this woman was very insulted which she had every right to be and of course, the director of our agency which was my supervisor's boss had to intervene, as she always did, by collaborating with this woman through email, in order to set up a best time for them to sit down and discuss the issue face to face, over lunch. Did my supervisor think for a moment that I was going to send this woman an email stating that, the miscommunication was solely my fault…No, let's not get it twisted; my mama didn't raise any fools.

Yes, my supervisor was known for this type of behavior quite often. This was her way of removing herself from any liabilities or any negative repercussions that would include her or would affect the program from being approved for the following and upcoming grants, since the program was a nonprofit and grant funded program. By me letting down my guards, **trusting** and confiding too much of myself and my experiences in Iraq to my supervisor, while in confidence in her office; thinking that she had good intentions for me and other Veterans, I believe she took advantage of my vulnerability.

For, I believed this and many other incidents was her way to use it against me to say that I was not mentally stable and that maybe the job was too much for me. Don't get me wrong, the job was find, and I was always capable to fulfill my duties as hired; it was just management.

Each morning that I reported to work, I had begun to dread it, for it reminded so much of the experiences I was subjected to while in Iraq; involving the mistreatment from the SFC, First Sergeant, Commanders and S-1's. Wow, I thought I was over all of that; I thought it had all been put behind me. I guess it wasn't; I was again, reliving the nightmare, the same hell that lead to my first mental break in Iraq.

Apparently, I was once again experiencing the misuse of authority, but now it was on civilian soil and I was also experiencing the physiological effects of decreased in appetite, insomnia, flashbacks of being taunted, similar to that, by my SFC/Commander/ S-1 and First Sergeant. Moreover, my migraines had even returned, for there was many times I thought my head was going to explode.

Slowly I was drifting into deep depression and although I continued to reach out to my support PTSD groups and presented to my scheduled individual therapy sessions, I knew my symptoms were not going to improve until I completely removed myself from the toxic work environment that I was presently in. Yet, I continued to ask myself, when is this misuse and abuse of authority ever going to stop?

My supervisor's misuse of authority continued for the entire six months that I remained employed with this agency. I guess as my punishment, which to this day I have no clue why she felt as though she had to abuse her authority; but whatever the reason and for the duration of my time employed with the agency I was assigned "grunt work" as she put it. Yes, she admitted and apologized for assigning me "grunt" work. Honesty, I believed that she enjoyed every bit of assigning me work that she didn't want to do, as though I was her personal assistant or secretary; which was not my title.

Nevertheless, each individual session I had with my Mental Health Professionals I would address my concerns, at which I was advised to request for a copy of my job description, which it later dawn on me that my supervisor had never given me, upon my initial hire; which she had forgotten to provide me. Therefore, when I requested a copy of my job description, it took her by surprised that I even asked, because she wasn't able to just provide me a copy, which was very strange. Moreover, when I received my job description it listed everything that I was "suppose" to be executing although I don't ever really recall providing case management services.

A matter of fact, I remember an incident where I attempted to provide case management services to a Veteran who had recently transitioned home, by linking this Veteran to various community veteran resources, but for some reason my supervisor had a problem with that. According to my supervisor she told me, "That isn't your job to provide case management."

Yet, at the start of me assisting this Veteran, she thought it was great; thereafter she complained that I was spending too much time providing this Veteran resources and peer support, although that was my title; Peer Support Specialist. Huh…Duh. This resulted in me becoming quite confused in what and why I was really hired.

In addition, my job description further included that I was to "develop and coordinate peer support/empowerment programs, including WRAP, (Wellness Recovery Action Planning), and peer-to-peer support groups; recruit, train and supervise volunteers to conduct peer support and empowerment programs; establish annual program goals and work plans; provide regular reports and evaluations as required regarding program status; coordinate activities with other community agencies and groups when necessary"; thus and on the contrary, **none of this I actually did.** All of this was simply bogus and was merely for grant and record purposes, so that it could be documented on paper that some of the grant funds were being allocated towards my job description. That was it!

I believe the real reason why she had such a difficult time providing me a copy of my job description when I inquired, was due to the fact that she never had one generated from the start. Therefore and for record, she had to quickly generate this bogus job description for my employee record and for the sake of the program, in order to continue to be grant eligible; since she didn't allow me to execute any of these jobs descriptions during the time that I was employed.

Furthermore, she always had a reason as to why I, in her eyes, **"was not ready"** to facilitate the wellness peer group, although I was already certified and had the appropriate training to do so. Yet there were other staff at this agency that had far less experience and definitely far less educational experience as I who held more responsibilities and held several groups, yet again, according to her, I "was not ready." No, I knew her angle and I knew exactly what she was trying to do. She was trying very hard to spark a negative response from me and because I knew this, I began to shut down at work, but I continued to seek support from my Mental Health Professionals at the local VA.

Moreover, I began to think about how am I or any Veteran expected to be able to move on in the civilian work environment if we're triggered day in and day out by those whom misuse and abuse their authority, especially if one of our past military traumas is the abuse of rank and power? How Ironic is that in today's working world…The only resolution is to become self-employed, which is something many Veterans are chosen to become.

15

Private Agency

Abuse of Novice Management Power & Control Reliving Triggers

After my ordeal with the non-profit agency I thought things would be different starting anew; especially working for a private agency, for I was wrong. Things had gotten worst. I soon began to question myself, "when am I ever going to get a break?" It was now four years that I've been home from Iraq, and although I've managed to advance in my education, obtaining and maintaining employment was becoming my greatest obstacle.

At the start of my employment with this agency it appeared that many of the staff were very warm and genuine, had a very close bond with one another; nevertheless the overall office environment was very team oriented. However, as in any work environment there is and will always be one who has to stand out from all the rest in management, to prove that he/she is most important or is doing more than all the rest. Yes, we had one of those. A matter of fact, towards the latter of my time with this employer, I experienced a couple of these types of individuals in management.

I truly was excited to work with this agency; for here I had an opportunity to be exposed to working with a different population of individuals which I graciously welcomed the challenge. At the start of my employment with this agency, I had even brought with me and shared my Veterans Information-Resource Handbook that I've been very well known at the local VA and my previous jobs for having, which I've compiled since my return from Iraq in 2005. Nevertheless, the previous management teams were very appreciative for the resources, for this agency at that time had very limited Veteran referrals and/or information to provide to their Veteran consumer population.

Things were going well; for I was even commended and "appreciated" for my "writing ability", until my excitement faded when management began to shift towards a power struggle and egos began to show its face within management. Yes, a few good supervisors/managers left the agency, leaving the rise to many novice individuals to be placed in management positions; whereby taking advantage of their titles by abusing their power and control.

Therefore and once again, the living hell that I was subjected to in Iraq was once again reoccurring in those in this novice management team. It was apparent, no matter what I did, no matter where I go, the recurrent events were continuously haunting me in my everyday life; but more so in my work environment through employers who were abusing their authority through berating and talking down at me, as well as other employees as though we were bodies without brains or a heart.

What was more appalling was that, many of the other employees were observant to the novice management's abuse of power and control, but said nothing, because they were afraid of losing their jobs. Yet, because I'd been subjected to this form of trauma first hand while in Iraq and because it was resulting in an ongoing trigger for me, it was now difficult for me to shun my face from it due to the fact that I wore my emotions on my face.

What has been most interesting to me is that prior to me being hired, my employer knew I was an Iraqi Veteran, knew I was a disabled Veteran, knew I was diagnosed PTSD; yet I was still hired, based on my educational background and work experience, and because I could bring Veteran experience and knowledge to the agency.

Now mind you, while employed with this agency I'd been commended many times for an "excellent job of gaining rapport" with the few Veterans whom I'd serviced.

Yet, I believe because I was beginning to receive too many commendations of a "job well done, excellent job, kudos," that a little jealousy was perhaps sparking the air from certain individuals, especially from those on this novice management team. I don't know. But, I didn't see anything wrong with me providing Peer to Peer Support; especially since I'd received the certified training to become a Peer Specialist through DBSA (Depression -Bipolar- Support-Alliance). Yet, often times I was reprimanded about and quote "sharing vet status" and that "conservative guidelines, re: therapist self-disclosure" would be reviewed with me.

Now, did this make any sense? No; my sentiments exactly. Many times management would speak to many of the employees as though they (staff) were the professors and employees were novice students. In other words, management were suppose to have been the ones with the book knowledge, yet employees appeared to have difficulty understanding or translating what was being conveyed; usually was not clearly articulated.

Then on another occasion I was told and quote, "Clearly you made an impression, but it is critical they understand there are multiple people in multiple organizations that can help them." Are you serious? Was this person actually saying this to me? First of all, I knew this already and I wasn't trying to put myself out there as if I was thee all who knew all. But, because I was the **only** Veteran employed with this agency, at the time that had **experienced war**, one would think that instead of this employer feeling **intimidated** by my knowledge and existence, this employer would have embraced it.

It was obvious, this employer had no idea the connection or even the camaraderie that Veterans have and will always share. Neither did this employer saw how much of an asset I could've been for the agency, as a Veteran.

Although I tried to explain that most Veterans feel most comfortable sharing their experiences with another Veteran, my expressed concern went on deaths ear. Besides, there were many times my counterparts couldn't and didn't have the type of resources available to provide to many of the Veterans whom they served. Honestly, it bothered me greatly, because I felt strongly in wanting to see that all Veterans received the information-resources that were due them, and not be cheated from receiving good information, solely because of some ego trip of management, whom decided that they wanted to compile their own agency rules and guidelines, which in my opinion were outraciously scrupulous and ridiculous, to say the least.

As a result, I no longer was sent out to see anymore Veteran Consumers and if I did, it was by coincidence.

Nevertheless, although this employer had a lot of knowledge when it came to the field, knowledge about the Veteran population wasn't at all in this agency's strong area. I say that to say this. If this employer had any knowledge about Veterans, then this agency would've known that Veterans whom been subjected to any form of trauma during war time have **"trust"** issues, and if that trauma involved authority abusing their power, then a trigger will occur.

That is what eventually happened with me involving this novice management team during the latter of my employment with this agency…

16

Private Agency PART-II

Hostile Work Environment; Triggers Continued Laid Off; the Best Thing That Could Have Happened & Bambooz'd; "Unfavorable for Hire"

The triggers continued as well as the hostile work environment. Day in and day out I felt as though I was walking on egg shells, became paranoid, couldn't trust anyone, and once again I felt as though I was reliving the experience I encountered while in Iraq, under the poor direction of the Unit Commander, First Sergeant and SFC. It was a dayshavoo moment. How could this be happening, again? I left a previous job and was triggered, because of a similar encounter to come to this and the same or similar situations were happening, regarding once again novice management abusing their authority.

I again began to ask myself? What is going on and why are these agencies hiring me knowing that I have PTSD, resulting in them being the cause of my trigger? Am I part of an experiment, to see if hiring a Veteran with PTSD is conducive to agency productivity? Did they hire me, so that it just looks good on their book, to show that they've hired a War Veteran? Or was it to try to prove that Veterans with PTSD are not mentally stabled, especially when they're intentionally provoked? What is it, because I can't seem to grasp the concept as to why these employers knowingly have hired me, a disabled Veteran with PTSD and yet have never tried to work with me towards a peaceful resolution; so that I would be able to maintain my employment status? Instead, they've aggravated the situation further, by continuously picking and meddling and using other employees to do the same; in other words, using moles to instigate the situations.

Yes, Moles within the agency. The closest thing I know about moles is what I see on television, but to observe it up close and personal within one's place of employment, it's sickening. What appeared, once upon a time, as a very close net team oriented environment became a very hostile work environment. Many of the staff whom I first meant upon my hire were no longer with the agency; therefore new hires were now being programmed, molded and placed to spy and report back to this novice management team about everything everyone were doing; from when and how long someone went to the bathroom, to when and how long someone took a break, to when and how long someone took lunch, to how someone spoke to a consumer on the phone. The moles behavior reminded me of the book I had to read, as a requirement for high school graduation titled, "1984", about Big Brother. It was pure ludicrous.

Street informants didn't have anything on many of these moles that were used at this agency. They were high-speed; they were on point, because they got many employees either fired or reprimanded, just for some asinine reporting.

I've never been known to want to treat anyone as a victim, instead I prefer to practice "empowerment" and "hope" as well as "responsibility" and "accountability"; whereby allowing individuals to explore within themselves areas in their lives that contributed to where they're currently are, then work on what they can do now to improve or correct their current situation and move forward. However, this approach to this novice management team and to many of the moles who listened in on many of my conversations to the consumers (clients) apparently was too "abrasive", which I was later confronted on, by this novice management supervisor. Are you serious?

Yet, this is one of the reasons why we have so many individuals who are so dependent on antidepressant medications, because their not given the appropriate tools for coping skills and healthy living, in order to help relieve them from a difficult situation.

No, I'm not referring to psychotropic medications, because that's in a class all by itself, because there are clients who may need their psychotropic medications to manage their psychosis symptoms. I'm referring for an example to individuals who instead of them managing their own household, their children are running the household and telling them what they will and will not do, or the woman who is allowing that man to live in her home whom he's unemployed and won't search for a job, yet she's stressing, or that elderly grandmother who is allowing her adult grandson to live with her, and doesn't want to help keep the house clean and is spending her social security check.

It was situations like this when I would encourage coping skills techniques, such as positive self-talk, being around supportive friends and family, incorporating meditation-yoga or some form of self-soothing activity; even music, art-work, journaling or writing poetry. Many times I would even explore with the consumer, by way of building their self-esteem and learning to set realistic boundaries and learning how and when to say, "No" and not feel bad, ashamed or guilty afterwards. However, although my approaches from my perspective were genuine and appropriate, it was never acceptable to this novice management team and supervisor, whom many of them had very little, if any, background mental health experience. And, if they did, it was from the classroom and textbooks, or through the modern day online degree program course.

Honestly, I believe the emotional abuse from this management team were simply from retaliation. I remember correctly, it all began when an incident occurred that involved a consumer, which resulted in an incident report having to be completed. However, because the incident report didn't exclude the responsible parties, which were the management team, I believe it resulted in retaliation from that point on from those on this management team. Twice were the incident report asked by management to be re-written and to exclude many of their names, as the responsible management personnel, whom failed to make themselves available to the field team when needed; and twice were the responsible parties names not excluded from the report. From that point on, it was dayshavoo again.

Yes, instead of being placed on the convoys back in Iraq, my writing ability was now being attacked as being "too judgmental." Yes, remember earlier I mentioned that I received commendation that my writing ability was well appreciated, well now after almost two years with this agency, all of a sudden my notes were now; according to management, "too judgmental."

Then, all of a sudden I had to meet with my novice manager/supervisor for what they called "supervision", which many times were a waste of mine and the agency's time, but then again it was this "power and control" issue that was going on within management. For some apparent reason they had to feel as though they had power; especially since I had now begun to shut down and was no longer talking with them. I didn't trust them, let alone trusted anyone within this agency. It was apparent, they weren't concerned about me; they were just nick picking, meddling and instigating, trying to get a negative response from me. Many times I felt as though I was in a twilight and didn't know who to trust and was afraid to talk to anyone, not knowing if they were going to misconstrue or take what I said out of context, which often times they did, anyway.

Furthermore, after this incident report and after this feeling of retaliation and feeling as though I was deliberately being attacked and not protected by management or anyone at the agency, my body went through some physiological changes. The same physiological symptoms occurred that began to creep up on me in Iraq and in my prior job was beginning to creep up on me again, at this job. Yes, the migraines, the insomnia, loss of appetite and difficulty concentrating. I soon began dreading to come to work.

No, I despised coming to work, I wanted so much to come to work to hear the news that certain individuals on the management team were either out sick, in the hospital or had either transferred or promoted out to another office out of state or that they had quit and found employment elsewhere. But, my luck never came. The thought was too good to be true.

Therefore, I knew in order for me to continue to remain employed I needed to take some time off and take a vacation. After all, I believed I had, at that time accumulated about seventy-two hours of vacation time. Nevertheless, when I requested to use my entire vacation time, for some reason word traveled throughout the agency that I was planning on leaving the agency; as a result, and up until the day that I took my vacation I was interrogated by management about whether I was planning to leave the agency. This harassment continued repeatedly.

Heck, who wasn't looking for at least some supplemental part-time employment while working for this agency. Honestly, there were many employees at this agency whom were looking for secondary employment; others were looking to actually leave the agency, all together, due to the mistreatment and daily harassment from senior management.

Consequently, every time we turned around our hours were being decreased from 40-32-30, and over time were no longer being allowed. The sad part of it all was that, employees were now being threatened to be fired if they were found intentionally accumulating overtime. That's how crazy and abusive this agency was being run by this management team. How were we able to live off of this type of hours, especially when many of us had families to support? I on the other hand, had a daughter in college who was my dependent. It was difficult to manage and pay my bills, but did they care? No, because management were receiving salary.

I recalled, word had spread throughout the agency about my supervisor leaving her Facebook page open on her computer, and on it she was sharing about how she just received a raise; meanwhile, the remaining of us whom were receiving hourly wages were struggling and barely making it. Yes, many of us were fueled, and I was one of them. I believed no-one could have been more fueled than I, for I had been evicted from my apartment, a few months prior.

During the time when my hours were decreased, it caused me to not be able to afford my rent which resulted in be being evicted. Yes, evicted. This was conveyed to the management team. Did they care? Were they concerned? No, of course not. Their income weren't being affected, because they were salary employees and they were guaranteed to go home to their families with food on their table and not worried about their lights being turned off, or being evicted. No, they had it made, and had no care in the world.

I will say this, had anyone offered me a full-time job with full benefits and salary pay, and to work in a drama less-free and non-hostile work environment during my vacation time off, heck yes! I would've been a dang fool to have turned it down. But I wasn't searching for employment on my vacation time off; I just needed a break away from this place, and these people. Anyway, I digressed...

From my knowledge, no-one was ever interrogated for requesting vacation time off, yet there were others whom had taken one and half week vacation time off, then when they returned, soon after, many had submitted their resignation. Yet, when I requested to take two weeks off it was as though I had committed a crime and management acted as though they were concerned about me exhausting all my vacation time all at once.

Huh, that's what they said...it all boiled down to "Power and Control"; they always wanted to know, **WHO-WHAT-WHEN-HOW-WHERE-WHY**. One would have thought I was working for a Communist Agency, because no-one was ever allowed to think for themselves, and Lord help us if we came up with a great idea for the agency...I'm surprised they never asked how long did we take for a pist...that's how much of a controlled environment it was.

Then, there was my shift change. This novice management team was very insensitive to many of the employees' family, let alone personal life or health; for they continued altering shifts and often times not collaborating with the employees beforehand, as did the previous management teams. From my recollection my shifts had been altered at least four times, yet there were new employees that were hired soon after me whom had been allowed to remain on their same shift since, they've been employed with this agency; or they were allowed to discuss which shifts would be appropriate and conducive to their personal and family schedules. In other words, there were always a selective few that were allowed to pick and choose which and how they wanted their shift to be arranged.

Moreover, I'd continuously addressed my issue with regards to it being imperative that my shift be consistent, due to my scheduled daytime doctor's appointments with my VA doctors as well as my schedule medication regiments. I clearly explained to them how difficult it was for me each time they abruptly altered my shifts, resulting in it affecting my medication regiments. I further explained that each time I have to alter my shift, my medication regiment as well has to be altered, which often times it effects the physiological changes in my body, due to having to constantly readjust to the different change in the time of day for me to take my medications. However, my concerns continuously fell on deaths ear; instead it was dismissed for I was still being insisted to move to a daytime shift or to return to the afternoon shift and to pick up some floating weekends overnights, which I declined to both.

Nevertheless, my concerned issues continued to fall on deaths ears, resulting in the increase of my anxiety, depression and recurrent events from Iraq that were playing back in my mind, day in and day out; causing me to avoid wanting to present to work. My sleep began to become effected, along with a decrease in my appetite, increase in headaches, difficulty concentrating and making decisions. As a result, everything that I was experiencing and with whom I was experiencing it with at work were always reported and shared with the appropriate personnel through the VA Healthcare System; my Therapist..

The best thing that ever happened was when I was called into the conference room after the end of my morning shift and was informed that the company was downsizing their overnight staff. I knew they were lying. Consequently, I believe this was their way of getting rid of me, because I wasn't willing to accept another shift change and because I had begun to shut down and was not communicating with them; and once again, dayshavoo…

Yes, because I wasn't willing to compromise my integrity by altering a report or accepting negligence on their behalf, I believe I was laid off as a form of retaliation. What for? I didn't owe them anything, neither did I trust them and they knew it. Furthermore, they knew the trust I once had when I entered this agency was gone forever and it was never going to return; no matter what they did or what they said. I could never trust them again. I lost all trust in this agency or even what this agency stood for. Sadly, they knew they had done wrong by me and had to do the right thing; besides they had no grounds for firing me and they knew it, for I had done nothing to give them reason, which is why they gave it a name, that I was being **"Laid Off."**

To see the look on their faces when they conveyed the news to me, and when they asked me to turn over my door key and I said, "Ok." For once in a long time, I had a sense of inner peace; for I knew this day was coming but I just didn't know when.

Honestly, I prayed for this day to come and it finally came. There was no fuss, no yelling, no disgruntle expressions on my part; although I'm quite certain that was what they were expecting, and I'm certain they probably had 911 on redial, to report of an out of control, disgruntle Veteran Employee. No, I didn't give them the benefit of the doubt. I'm sure I disappointed their outcome of what they were hoping to expect, as well as their perception of a Veteran with PTSD.

That's what's so sad about society. Too often, us Veterans with PTSD are generalized and perceived as **"out of control, a ticking time bomb"** or that we're not able to rationalize and walk away. It seems as though, we're being set up to fail in many cases. Good examples are the two agencies that hired me. Both hired me, because I was a Veteran. Yet, both intentionally provoked me, just to see how I was going to respond. Although I was one of those Veterans who had the capability to rationalize and keep my composure, as well as sought out professional and supportive help from my VA Professionals, families and friends, there are Veterans who are not me and given the same situation wouldn't have even blinked twice and the outcome wouldn't had been a good one, but may had been fatal for everyone involved.

Ok, they can call it what they like...But it is what it is and I'm most thankful that I no longer have to punch their clock and I hope my **Veterans Resource Handbook**, which a copy was provided to one of their daytime employees will be utilized by all their staff, in order to help the Veterans in the community.

On that day, I had mixed emotions; I was angry and I was relieved. I was angry that I no longer had a job, and worried about how I was going to pay my bills; yet, I was relieved, because I was slipping back into that dark place and I was afraid of myself; my thoughts; even my possible actions.

On my drive home, millions of dark thoughts clouded my mind; I couldn't wait to get home; I needed to call my therapist; I needed to let her know what happened; I needed to share with her the news.

I can't recall if she picked up on the first ring, or if I left a message. Anyway, when I did speak with her, hearing her voice was a relief; she agreed that it was the best thing that could've happened... We talked for awhile, and I felt better and agreed that it was the best thing for me, to no longer be employed with this employer; due to the hostile work environment that I was subjected to; it was unhealthy for me...

Therefore, I was satisfied with the outcome, for it was my time to leave, to move on, and to pursue larger and aspiring ventures. But most importantly, I was able to walk away with my Sanity and Dignity. Hence, I thought this too, would be another chapter of a page for me to turn, so that I would be able to move on, but and again, I was wrong...

Now, although I was "laid off"; so, I was told. And, although three months had gone by and I was receiving unemployment, something wasn't right. I couldn't understand why, a person with three college degrees, and a disabled Iraqi veteran was being turned down for employment and clearly for positions that I was fully qualified for. Well, inquiry no more.

I later discovered that this same employer had conveyed to a prospective employer, whom I actually was given a start date and time to begin work, that I was **"Unfavorable for Hire."** Are you Serious? Yes, I couldn't believe what I was being told, by this prospected employer, which was the reason he couldn't allow me to begin work. To add insult to injury, this prospective employer continued to state that, this revelation came about, not by him, but according to him, he doesn't

"have the last say-so", yet he conveyed that his H.R. Department who conducted the background check with my previous employer reported that I **"would not be fit for the team."** Wow, there's that word "team" again. That sounds exactly like something this previous employer would say.

The problem I've faced since returning from Iraq is not allowing myself to grow close to anyone; for every time that I do, or every time that I let down my guards; whether with new people whom I meet, or new co-workers in the work place, or allow myself to confide anything of myself to co-workers or supervisors, or even make an attempt to expand my social network, it never fail, these individuals whom I allow in my circle "always" become disloyal and cannot be trusted. Which many times result in me, shutting down and remaining focused on only the task, or the mission at hand, and nothing more; especially since I'd been subjected to poor leadership in Iraq; it actually was an eye-opener, in that it taught me "Trust No-one"; not even family, for family tend to talk about and gossip what they don't understand.

The only thing I want to do is, go to work; do my job; then return home; and many times, be left alone. I don't care about being friends with co-workers; going out to lunch with co-workers; neither do I care to partake in company holiday parties and social gatherings. Does that make me not a Team Player? Or does it simply mean that I'm a Veteran trying to live day to day; to manage her PTSD?

Nevertheless, this incident was immediately reported to the appropriate personnel, with the Veteran and Workforce Agency to investigate, so that this wouldn't continue to happen, and interfere with my future job prospects; therefore I contacted the Department of Labor. After speaking with the Department of Labor, it was explained that, had I been fired due to "Unfavorable for Hire" or because of any "Insubordination of Behavior" I currently wouldn't be eligible to receive any unemployment compensation benefits. As an end result and conversation, I proceeded to contact an attorney to take the necessary legal steps for filing suit for slander.

Wow, I find it quite interesting how people, whether in the Civilian sector or in the Military thrive and feed on "Power and

Control." Honestly, I feel sorry for this population of people, because I only imagine what they were subjected in their childhood or lack thereof; resulting in them projecting this senseless behavior towards others, not realizing that their fight and struggle is not with the person on the opposite end, but it's with the person who they see in the mirror.

17

Therapist Relocated

Reassigned Therapist (Psychologist); No Connection - No Rapport

I had built a good and trusting rapport with my therapist and prior to her leaving she had briefly informed me about my new therapist, which I already knew I wasn't going to be satisfied. Well, when my scheduled appointment arrived I presented and met my new therapist. For record, she was a Psychologist and not a Psychiatrist, which is a huge difference. Too often I have heard many say that a Psychiatrist doesn't provide counseling, and only prescribe medications. That's not exactly true. It all depends on the professional and what service they're willing to provide. With regards to my previous therapist, not only did she prescribe my medications, but I received the two in one treatment.

Nevertheless, this new therapist's personality appeared to be very disconnected. I would've had a better chance talking to a tree than with her. Upon entering she immediately began the session by handing me a clip board and instructed that I take the Beck Depression test (BDI-II). The Beck Depression test measured the intensity, severity and the depth of my depression. No brief introduction of herself, her educational background, or even how long she's been working with the Veteran population; nothing. She didn't even discuss with me my trauma experience that occurred in Iraq; nothing. No rapport;

no connection; no empathy. No feeling of genuineness; how I'm doing, how's school, how's the adjustment and transition been going? Heck, I wouldn't had been upset if she'd asked how was the weather; something. She didn't even ask if there were any changes in my sleep or eating patterns; or any recent family or personal crisis; nothing. Was she serious?

During this same time I was also a graduate student in a Counseling program and was actually taking a psychological appraisal course. There was no way I felt comfortable taking this test, for I believed the answers would've been compromised. Therefore, I told her that I'd rather just talk to her, instead. Besides, I was trying to give this woman a chance, although I already had my preconceived feeling about her.

Well, the session didn't go well. Consequently, I found it quite interesting that this psychologist apparently didn't take the time to familiarize herself with my mental health history, because had she; prior to seeing me, she wouldn't had to ask me many of the questions that she did. Moreover, with every response that I provided her, in return her inquiries were condescending, sarcastic and many times judgmental. I felt as if I was being blamed by her, for what happened to me in Iraq.

Often times during the sessions, after she would make a judgmental inquiry, I would say to her, "if you had taken the time to read the mental health history, you would've known what lead up to that."

Of course she didn't appreciate me telling her how to do her job. But she needed to be told. I actually felt as if this woman was cutting me to shreds, by making statements without even knowing the entire story, just because she was too busy or too lazy to familiarize herself with the case notes, prior to my appointment, as did my previous therapist.

If I remember correctly, I ended in the middle of our session. I honestly conveyed to her, "This isn't going to work for me", for I didn't feel any connection between she and I. Neither did I foresee that there were ever going to be a connection, due to our first meeting. Our personalities were not gelling and I felt very uncomfortable, irritable and very angry throughout the session.

One thing for certain in which I observed was how often she folded her arms, periods throughout the session. In other words, I was very cognizant of this therapist non-verbal, as well as her verbal. I knew she was not the therapist for me; therefore I got up and walked out of the session.

Before I left the building, I remembered there was another therapist, who was a Psychiatrist and whom I had seen when my previous therapist was on maternity leave. This therapist also was familiar with my case, therefore I addressed my concerns to the secretary and requested that I be assigned to that particular therapist, which I was. Thereafter, I was then provided my next scheduled appointment with my requested assigned therapist...

Too often Veterans have left the VA Healthcare System, entirely because of being dissatisfied with the services from either their mental health or their medical providers, not knowing that they have the right to request for another provider if they believe that they're not receiving quality services. As you notice, I didn't say **"adequate"** service, but I did say **"quality"** service.

As a Veteran, **Quality = Excellence** and **Adequate is never good enough.**

18

Resident VA Staff (Third Year Medical Residents)

Veteran's Choice - Unprofessional VA Administrative Staff

One thing I've found to be very upsetting when receiving services at the local VA is when I've had a scheduled appointment to see my orthopedic or pain doctor and instead, walks in a third year resident student who introduces themselves and tell me that they will be my doctor for that day. That is not acceptable. Too often I've spoken to many Veterans whom have expressed this same outrage of not being given the choice to be seen by their own doctor but, instead is forced to be seen by a third year resident student. I used the word **"forced"**, although the word forced may seem a bit extreme, but often times the medical staff will try to convince Veterans that the third year medical student is qualified to perform the duties, to provide care to us.

As Veterans, we're not saying that the third year medical students are not qualified to perform their duties; however what we're saying is, we as Veterans should be given a **"CHOICE"** if we want to be serviced by a third year medical student, opposed to being seen by our actual primary care providers, upon our scheduled visits to the VA. Of course the response from the staff is, "They're considered a doctor, too and they're being supervised." On the contrary, that's not good enough for many of us Veterans whose disability compensation depends on accuracy and consistency of progress notes.

Many Veterans, including myself believe that often times these residents don't take the time to read our medical and/or mental health history, prior to seeing us; in order to know how or what type of approach to use when they speak to us, which often times result in verbal altercations between the resident students and the Veterans, as well as misdiagnosing our condition. Also, it has been observed by Veterans that many of these residence attitudes are very cocky, arrogant and very condescending, to say the least. Many of these residents comes from various local universities and abroad and very few have bed-side manners to even take the time to ask, "How are you doing, today" or "Did you have a safe travel."

In short, Veterans including myself would like to have a choice as to whether we want to be serviced by a resident student or by our assigned doctor. I find that it is very inconsiderate when I'm not notified in advance when my doctor will not be present for my scheduled appointment, then to show up later to discover that my doctor will not be seeing me, but that I will be seen by a resident; especially when I have driven thirty-forty minutes to my appointment or maybe had cancelled a prior appointment so that I could attend this appointment. Same thing applies to other Veterans, who may have traveled two, three maybe more hours and feeling the same way.

It doesn't take but a few seconds to send out letters or pick up a phone to notify that the doctor has cancelled the appointment and would like to reschedule or to extend to us a choice if we would like to be seen by an alternate doctor, which could be a resident student. Again, that should be our choice; after all, it is our bodies, our lives and our compensations that are being effected.

Then, there's the administrative staff. Wow, where do I begin?

Now, don't get me wrong, but I've been to various Veteran Hospitals where the administrative staffs are very warm and professional, like the one I currently attend. Then, there are those whom you wonder where in the world did the HR (Human Resource Department) discover and hire these employees.

What have been conveyed to me in such frustration, by many Veterans are the behaviors and the attitudes they receive from many of the unprofessional clerks at surrounding Veteran Hospitals; according to some Veterans, those "million dollar attitudes, that doesn't have pots to piss in or windows to throw it out of". According to many Veterans, few of these clerks sit behind their counters talking about their personal business for all to hear; like we really want to hear them air out their dirty laundry in the public, whether they're male or female clerks. No, we really don't care to know what's going on in your homes. Trust me, us Veterans have our own traumas, we don't need to hear yours.

What bothers me the most and have been shared by other Veterans is that, some of these clerks are Veterans themselves; therefore, they aught to know better, yet they've become too complacent and selfish. On the other hand, the others are civilian, whom just doesn't know any better, because they have never worked with our population, or have never acquired the importance or the honor of servicing our population.

Overall, many of these clerks have been witnessed forever chewing their gums until the cows come home, while ignoring Veterans (us) when we approach the counter for service. Little do they realize, without the services from Veterans, they wouldn't have a job.

As we say in the military…**You Need To Stay In Your Lane!"**

19

Struggling and Transitioning Home

Local Non-Profit Charitable and Church Organizations & Available Resources for Veterans

After my deployment I never thought I would be the one to have to struggle to obtain employment or even with finances, but I did. Prior to being deployed I'd joined and became a member to a very prominent local church, whom I reached out to for financial help, which to my surprised resulted in a total insult of being offered $150 towards rent that was $850, at that time. Wow, not only was it an insult, but I couldn't believe that I was only being offered $150, even after I explained that I was a member, a returning Iraqi Veteran as well as my situation of being given an eviction notice to vacate the premises within ten days. Nevertheless, I decided not to accept the $150 offer. I became angry; felt betrayed, which resulted in me not returning to affiliate or fellowship with that church, or any church.

Despite the negative many may say about living on the East Coast; however just like with any place, there are its advantages and its disadvantages. Although being a Native New Yorker, the advantage of being from the East Coast is its diverse culture, food and art exhibits; more importantly, fellowshipping at the local churches. One thing for certain about the local churches in the East Coast is that, not only do they take care for their member's needs, but they take care of any one who present in dyer needs. It's never about numbers; it's never about gratification or glorification from the public. I shared that to say this, no prominent church is bigger or, no Elder, Minister, Pastor, Bishop, or Pope is more prominent or powerful than God and God will have the last say so, in how these individuals treat those whom come to them for help.

After which, I sought financial help from local non-profit charitable organization, as well as other local church organizations, however many of them were only able to offer $50 towards rent and/or would pay the utility bill, provided that I had proof of a notice of "no service or turn off "of utilities. This never made any sense to me, because why would a person wait until their utilities were turned off to receive help? The system never makes any sense to me and it makes it even more difficult and very frustrating for Veterans trying to transition to function in an already chaotic environment.

Nevertheless, since my utilities were not turned off I was offered $50 towards my rent, which again I decided not to accept, because I knew I was still $800 away from the total amount needed for my rent and I had no idea where or by whom I was going to gather the remaining portion of funds.

As an end result, I had a very hardworking and helpful OIF/OEF Social Worker who was able to assist by linking me into emergency financial services through various Veteran organizations. Many of these organizations had helped me throughout my transitioning period with regards to, vehicle repairs, rent and utility payments, phone bills, automobile payments and automobile insurance. These organizations allowed me to be able to mentally function and not have to stress or worry about being evicted; neither was I hindered from attending school, due to an inoperable vehicle. I will always be thankful and grateful to these Veteran organizations, which many Veterans are not aware of the resources available to them, even to this day.

Moreover, I've had the opportunity to collaborate with other Veteran colleagues who've expressed their frustration with regards to many non-profit charitable and church organizations. One Veteran asked me if I would mention in this book, "Why are these local charity churches more willing" to help other individuals who are not legal citizens with housing and emergency funding; "opposed to Veterans?" But of course, this was before this Veteran knew about the many Veteran organizations that provides emergency financial assistance. But even so, because of his lack of knowledge and resource of information, at that time, he had every right to feel and to express how he felt.

After my financial ordeal and I was able to recover, I took it upon myself to compile a **"Veteran Resource Handbook"** which I previously mentioned in the earlier chapters, and of which I've been very well known for; wherever I've gone, i.e. workplaces or even volunteer at the local VA. Moreover, a copy was even left with a co-worker at my last place of employment; although a personal binder was initially made when I was hired with this former employer, which prior to my lay off, the binder was no longer able to be located. This project is and will always be my signature work for Veterans everywhere. There are more and more available financial resources for Veterans, yet many Veterans are not aware. Why is it?

It seems as though unless a Veteran knows someone who knows someone on the **"inside"** with the information, a Veteran will never be privileged to receive available and important information. Some Veterans are made aware; others never are made aware and miss out on very pertinent information that often times can help either their compensation or just having the knowledge about their illness. For some, the information arrive too late, resulting in progression or even exasperate in their treatment; resulting in many Veterans resorting to suicide.

On a flip side, there are too many homeless Veterans living in shelters, on the streets, under bridges, in their vehicles, and living between homes, such as living with a different friend a night. Some, such as Adult Protect Services would probably define a home as a roof over one's head. Well, us Veterans define a home as one that we have mail that is delivered to us in our names; one that we have a key to; one that we are the king or queen to our own domain and can throw anyone out of whom are not welcomed. That is what we define as our home. Yes, from my knowledge there are some transitional homes for Veterans, but very few are even mentioned and/or regulated appropriately.

20

Memoir: Service Connected Injuries Appeals

A decision on my claim for service connected compensation was received on June 14, 2005 and that was for my PTSD with a 0 percent rating for one of the injuries which I sustained in January 2005; service medical records supported this injury.

On 6 July 2005, I received a letter from my local Veterans Hospital informing me that a "careful review of my examination results, including laboratory testing has been carried out except for the previously recorded or reported problems, no new or pertinent findings have been identified from this most recent evaluation...this examination does not automatically initiate a claim for VA benefits. If you wish to file a claim, please contact a Veteran Benefit Counselor." Therefore, I proceeded to file claims for my service connected injuries that I sustained, while in Iraq, whether major or minor.

Appeal #1:

My C&P (Compensation & Pension) examinations for my physical injuries were a nightmare, for it seemed as though I was being examined by what I described as "almost in the grave" physicians whom should had been retired 10-years priors; if you ask me. Yes, my C& P Physicians appeared to have been what would have been the last of the World War I Physicians. Anyways, go figure; my claim ended up being denied. Yes, all of my injuries that I presented and had supportive documentation, such as LOD (Line of Duty) supportive documentation of injuries, were denied; according to what "they" say "based on all the evidence of record", dated 6 January 2006. On 24 January 2006, a NOD (Notice of Disagreement) was also received in the regional office. On 1 February 2006 I began receiving what all of us Veterans are all too familiar with...yes, the electronic print-out that states **"We have received your application for benefits or we are still processing your application for compensation..."**

Nevertheless, along with my previous package, it highlighted that on 16 April 2006 I received a notice stating that, "since no response was received, the appeal will follow the traditional process"; which I never recalled receiving. Anyway, it continued to state, "this statement of the case will serve as notification of that action." I had no idea what was about to happen or what was going on with my case and/or soon to be appeals.

Too often, because Veterans are unfamiliar with the process of filing for compensation and benefits claims, many of our claims get lost in the system or go unnoticed; which result in many Veterans becoming disappointed, aggravated and angry with the VA system.

Moreover, I continued to receive the electronic notices about my **"application for benefits"** being received, 13 July 2006. Thereafter, on 20 November 2006 I received a letter from Regional informing me that my certified appeal had been received and that my VA records were being transferred to the Board in Washington, D.C.; at which, the board will notify me when they have received my records.

Appeal #2:

My service connected Injuries continue to be denied. On 10 November 2008 my claim was received to the appropriate destination, and once again, I received the electronic notice **"application for benefits"** have been received**,** on 14 November 2008. Soon after, I received another electronic notice on 12 January 2009, stating that **"we are still processing your application for compensation."** Thereafter, on 16 January 2009 my claim was considered based on all evidence of record, and on 26 January 2009 according to their record, I was notified of this decision.

Throughout this appeal process, I continued to receive electronic notices; on 3 February

2009 I received a noticed stating that an **"application for benefits"** has been received.

On 23 March 2009, per record, a claim was reconsidered based upon additional evidence received, as well as the other evidence of record. Then, on 31 March 2009 I submitted a NOD (Notice of Disagreement); which was received by the appropriate personnel. Thereafter, I received another electronic notice on 17 April 2009 that my **"application for benefits"** has been received. On 26 September 2009 De Novo Review performed based on all evidence of record.

Appeal #3:

My service connected Injuries continue to be denied. On 28 September 2009, by their report, I received a "Statement of the Case" outlining actions taken on my claim. As such, on 22 October 2009 a Substantive Appeal was received. All the while, I was undergoing various ongoing physical therapy treatments, i.e. desensitization, paraffin treatments; receiving X-rays, Cat-Scans, and an EMG (Electromyogram). The purpose of the electromyogram was to detect any abnormalities of electrical activity of muscle, which can occur in cases involving muscles inflammation, pinched nerves, muscle dystrophy, and peripheral nerve damage. In addition, a consult for a C&P at another Veteran Hospital was conducted, on 12 January 2010. Soon after, I received another electronic notice on 24 February 2010, that my **"application for benefits"** has been received. Following my C&P procedure, **On 17 May 2010 the claim was considered based on all the evidence of record.**

According to record, the service connection of the first injury was granted with a percentage effective 10 November 2008, the other, effective 12 January 2010; although both injuries were considered, in my eyes, from the same family of extremities and were injured on the same day in question.

Although I had finally been compensated for my service-connected injury, which I sustained in 2004, my fight was not over; neither was I satisfied with the rating outcome, due to how this particular injury had, has and will continue to affect me in my daily physical functioning and mobility. And, although I was granted for **one** of my service connected injury, I continued to be denied other injuries which I sustained. Therefore, my appeals and my fight continued.

On 18 May 2010 the electronic notices continued to arrive, stating, **"Application for benefits"** has been received. Thereafter, other notices followed; on 2 December 2010, then another on 4 January 2011 and still my fight and appeals continued...

21

Memoir

DAV (Disabled American Veterans) There to Help Veterans; Starting Over Being Respected, Appreciated and Not Dismissed VES (Veterans Evaluation Services)

Throughout my appeal process, the DAV (Disabled American Veterans) has been very helpful, in advocating on my behalf. If I can remember correctly, their intervention began when they were appointed as my authorized representative. As my authorized representative they submitted materials as a claim, in support for the service connected injuries, which I was claiming entitlement. For each appeal and intervention made on my behalf, the DAV always kept me informed, either by "cc" on correspondence or by a letter of notification of actions made, re: my benefits.

* **First letter received:** Authorized Representation, 7 November 2008
* **Second letter received:** Material sent, in support of the pending claim for benefits by the Department of Veteran Affairs; 22 January 2009
* **Third letter received:** Notification of service connected injuries denied; 26 January 2009. A NOD (Notice of Disagreement) process was explained in the letter.

- **Fourth letter received:** re: NOD decision, dated 26 January 2009. Appeal Initiated.
- **Fifth letter received:** 21 October 2009. Pending Appeal.
- **Sixth letter received:** 13 November 2009. Pending Appeal.
- **Seventh letter received:** 20 July 2010; of unofficial notification of service connected injury being granted. A NOD (Notice of Disagreement) process was also explained in this letter.
- Eighth **letter received:** 26 October 2010 of the "Statement of Accredited Representative in Appeal Case", which was prepared on my behalf, due to ongoing symptoms from service connected injuries.
- Ninth **letter received:** 2 November 2010; per my copy for service connected increase request, per injury granted 20 July 2010.
- Tenth **letter received:** 14 February 2011; informing me that they were still working on my claim for my service connected injury increase; that was granted 20 July 2010.

Required documents to be completed were submitted to DAV Authorized Representative in person on 28 February 2011.

It appeared as though my voice was finally being heard, with regards to my symptoms and no longer did I feel ignored. I soon began to be further evaluated by another outside source; MES Solutions. MES Solutions is a Veterans Evaluation Service.

Moreover, new x-rays were being performed on 24 February 2011; thereafter I immediately received a follow up diagnostic appointment to see the physician on the following day, 25 February 2011. During my visit with this physician, I finally felt respected, appreciated and that my symptoms were not being dismissed, but that they were being validated; neither did I feel pressured to accept taking pain medications for the rest of my life, resulting in eventually becoming addicted to the pain medications, which too often, many Veterans does.

Meanwhile, although I was being assessed and evaluated ongoing for my service connected physical injuries, I continued to suffer with day to day triggers of trying to manage my PTSD; which was also spilling over and effecting me on my job and as a result, I received an appointment on 28 April 2011 with MES Solutions, for a PTSD evaluation for a disability increase. Nevertheless, I had now received two electronic notices; one on 2 March 2011 and another following 3 May 2011, stating **"We are still processing your application for compensation."**

4 May 2011, I submitted the required documents to my DAV Authorized Representative via Express Delivery, for continual supportive claim in the ongoing appeal case, re: my service connected injuries. Thereafter, on 9 May 2011 I received a confirmation notice from my DAV Accredited Representative, that the submitted materials in question had been submitted in support of the pending claim for benefits; although my battle continues to be compensated for my service connection injuries.

As previously stated, too often Veterans have given up the fight to be compensated for what is due them, for injuries they have sustained while serving their Country, whether major or minor, whether mental or medical; but regardless the form of injury, a Veteran should never be denied compensation for any injury sustained while serving his or her Country...

22

Diagnosis

Unsure (Misdiagnosis) Not being heard Masking the Underlying Problem; Instead, Being Prescribed Pain Medications

Aggravation was an understatement, to describe how I was feeling towards this particular team of doctors at the initial local Veterans Hospital. Each time I presented for my appointment to be examined for a follow-up, it was always the same questions being asked of me, i.e. "On a scale from one to ten what is your level of pain?" At the start of my visits and throughout, my responses were always either "a ten" or "off the scale". This team of doctors appeared as though they could not understand my level or magnitude of pain; yet they were always adamant on prescribing me pain medications to mask the underlying problem; instead of taking the time to probe a little deeper in discovering what was causing me to be in such high sensitivity to pain.

Nevertheless, with every visit I became more frustrated, aggravated, irritated and all the words that end with "ated", that one can imagine. I became appalled at how unsure this team of doctors appeared to be in diagnosing my injury. My right wrist was one of my injuries in question, which was misdiagnosed about four to five times, before they actually got it right; even after several x-rays, test, and examinations were performed as well as me advocating and voicing for myself. I'd even requested to have surgery to correct my injury, although I was informed many times that, due to the time that had lapse with regards to the injury, having surgery would only exasperate the problem; therefore, surgery was not recommended.

To add insult to injury, upon my return from deployment, I submitted "ALL" my LODs (Line of Duty) supportive documents to my local VA hospital for record, and for the purpose of filing my claims. One would think that the supportive documents I submitted would, not only assist these doctors in making their jobs easier, with diagnosing and quickly repairing my injury; but apparently, it became a living &#*^ for me daily; living with chronic pain.

First, my LOD's initially were never submitted to the rating/compensation board; so they said. Either my LODs were submitted, but were misplaced, accidently overlooked or simply disregarded; either way, the continuous prescribing of pain medications were only masking the root of the problem.

Whatever the reason, by this time, it was now about five years that I'd been home from Iraq and five years that I've been living with ongoing, day to day, excruciating pain and more and more I was feeling helpless and believed, as though I was not being heard by this team of doctors; whom I relied on to provide me with an accurate diagnosis, so that I would know what I was working with, and would know how to better manage my own condition. Hence, because they had no clue as to what my injury diagnosis was, they were not able to accurately diagnose me properly; which resulted in them continuously prescribing me various pain medications that only caused me heavy and daily sedations.

Because of the line of work I was employed doing at the time, I addressed my concerns with this team of doctors; explaining that it is very difficult for me to perform my job duties, while still feeling the lethargic effects from the medications. Therefore, I was provided an alternative to the medications, by taking the medications after work and before I go to sleep. Well, after trying that approach, the effects were even worst, because I appeared very lethargic amongst my co-workers, even towards the consumers whom I were interacting with.

Again my concerns were addressed with this team of doctors,

who presented another alternative approach, which was to increase my dosage, but to begin me on a very small dosage for the first one to two weeks, then increase the dosage thereafter about the third to fourth week; by that time my body "should" become adjusted to the medications, which would lessen the lethargic and sedation effects. Yeah Right! That didn't happen, either. Again, my concerns were addressed to this team of doctors, which I guess their hands were tied, because whatever pain medications they prescribed the same effects happened.

My experience with this team of doctors was apparently not a pleasant one, neither was it satisfying, to say the least. I've spoken to many Veterans whom had similar, if not the same experience, in which I've encountered; maybe not with this team of doctors, but with other doctors who didn't take the time to probe further; but appeared to be more adamant in prescribing them pain medications, instead of being more concerned in finding out how to actually correct the Veterans underlying issue(s).

Many Veterans have shared that as a result of being placed on pain medications, instead of being offered other alternative treatments, many had become addicted to their pain medications; whereby others made overdose (OD) attempts, not so much to intentionally end their lives, but just to stop their pain."

23

False Alarm

Statement Taken Out of Context

I continued to suffer being in pain, daily and no-one seemed to be able to help me; instead I continued to be instructed to take the pain medications and was denied surgery and was informed that no surgery could repair my injury. This was something I was not ready for, neither was I willing to hear, nor accept. I wasn't willing to accept the thought of allowing my body to depend on pain medications for the rest of my life. That, was **UNACCEPTABLE**; that, was not about to happen, not in this life time. In other words, I was basically being instructed to accept what I was being told, and don't ask any questions…**Not! I Don't Think So!**

Well, anyone who has ever been in such excruciating pain, to the point where you want to just hurt someone; just so that you can just stop hurting, well, that's the type of pain I always was experiencing, from day to day. My pain was chronic and ongoing. If someone looked at me the wrong way, I wanted to just physically hurt them; if someone said something to me that I believe that was a stupid comment, I wanted to physically hurt them, just because I believed that they were stupid enough to open their mouth and form such a stupid gesture. That's how much I believed that the only way I would be able to release my physical pain, would be to add physical pain to someone else. No, I wasn't thinking rationally; the level of pain that

I was experiencing wouldn't allow me to even see clearly, let alone think rationally.

Well, on this particular day I started out being very excited, because I had prior been examined, upon a second opinion consult, by a physician who was brought in from outside. This physician had made a recommendation that my injury was suitable for surgery. I was finally relieved and very happy, that after all these years I was finally going to have my injury repaired. However, after I wasted my time presenting to my scheduled pre-op appointment, and believing that there was a possibility that I may be able to have the surgery, I later discovered upon my return that the outside doctor who examined me had not returned, but had returned to his home state (unknown); however, I remember this surgeon mentioning that he was from the East Coast, but I don't remember which state. Anyway, my surgery was not going to happen, because there was no other surgeon licensed at this particular clinic to perform my surgery, at that time, so I was told.

Nevertheless, I was informed that this particular surgeon was not going to perform my surgery at the VA Hospital, anyway; instead, it was going to be performed at the surgeon's local hospital where he was practicing out of; which was a local medical facility near the VA hospital. In other words, I received so many conflicting stories and bogus reasons as to why my surgery was not carried out. Many times I believed I was talking to a bunch of Politicians, instead of doctors, because I could never get a straight or accurate response out of anyone, re: my surgery or what was going. How convenient!

At this point I became so angry that I just wanted to pick up the furniture and just throw it across the room; I was angry at anyone that even resembled a doctor. Thoughts began to go through my mind, on how other Veterans were treated. I never understood when I would witness other Veterans becoming upset, angry, yelling, and cussing at the staff and the doctors; until now. Now, I understood why?

I was finally experiencing how it felt to be not heard, to be dismissed, to be mistreated, to be lied to, to be betrayed, to be just a number, to be unimportant, to be just another patient on the list. I was beyond furious; I was beyond fueled. I had now become unreasoning raged.

Because I was so raged I went to address my concerns to a patient advocate. During my conversation, I cried and was so intensely rage, at which I made a comment stating, "I understand why Veterans give up mentally and physically, in fighting for their appeals and compensations; I see and understand why now; because, they get tired of not being heard and fighting with a system that doesn't listen to them; and like me, I'm tired of fighting; I'm getting tired of fighting, too; I'm in pain; I've been in pain since 2004; I've been in pain for the last six years and I'm tired of being in pain; I don't want to keep taking pain medications, I want them to fix the problem, but they're not listening to me."

After these statements were made, I was then asked whether I have any weapons at home and if I was going to try to harm myself. First of all, I couldn't understand what my comment or statements had to do with what type of weapons I had or didn't have at home. But anyway, I didn't think anything further about it, so my response was, Yes, I have a .38 Special, what Veteran doesn't have any weapons at home? Then she asked, "Do you plan on harming yourself." What? What the….. I began to ask myself, what does that have to do with the cost of peanuts, and where is this woman going with these questions? So, I responded to her, if I was going to take my life it would've been done a long time ago, but I have a daughter in college who needs me; I want to see her graduate, get married have a family, and become successful; she's what keeps me living for another day so, I have something and someone to live for.

At this point I became curious to her next question…

Apparently, that wasn't good enough, because before I knew it, this individual deceived me, by having me to believe that I was going to be administered cortisone injection to relieve my pain, by stating that she had already called over to the ER and that they were expecting me; but instead, I was again betrayed and lied to.

After I walked over to the ER, next thing I knew I was speaking to Social Workers and then was told that I couldn't leave until a Psychologist came down to speak with me. A What? At that point I began to put 2+2 together and realized what was about to happen. Yes, apparently, my statements had been taken out of context, as that of Suicidal Ideations, which my statements were never intended as such. They were only statements made from expressing ones emotional frustrations.

Moreover, I was detained and locked in one of the ER rooms, against my will. Although I'd pleaded with the ER Staff that I was not suicidal, neither did I express any intent or plan to end my life; thus, the ER staff continued to deny me exit. After several failed attempts to exit the ER, the window of opportunity for my escape finally arrived when the ER staffs were distracted.

Consequently, I noticed that the only exit from the ER into the lobby and front entrance of the VA was to enter an employee ID code, on a wall key pad; adjacent the nurses' station. Therefore, I knew that I didn't have access to this code, so I hid in a doorway, as if I was a visiting relative of another Veteran (Patient); so that when a doctor , who wasn't familiar with who I was, would assume that I was a family member waiting for someone to open the door, at which I would exit. Well, that's exactly what happened; after continuously ducking and hiding several times before the opportunity to run for freedom.

After I ran through the door, I immediately stopped running, and then quickly walked briskly trying not to bring any attention to myself and certainly not wanting to alarm security that I (Patient-Veteran) had escaped from ER-alleged suicidal watch. As I walked to my vehicle, I prayed that I was not caught; I was scared; I was shaking; I was nervous. I began thinking, if I wasn't a criminal it sure as heck felt as though I was one. I quickly entered my car, sat for a moment to allow my body and my mind to become in sync; I knew I needed to calm my breathing and my heart before starting my vehicle.

I then proceeded to leave the VA facility; however I drove around for a while, before going home, fearing that the ER would've contacted the police to meet me at my home, in order to return me to the VA hospital. After about one and half hours I finally arrived home, locked my door and prayed that the police wouldn't come knocking on my door

The moral to this is, as a Veteran I was **betrayed, and deceived** by a VA Staff whom I expressed emotional frustration to, in a time when I was in excruciating, chronic, ongoing pain. Yet, my comment and/or statement expressed were taken out of context. This leaves me to wonder, if this happened to me, how many other Veterans have this happened to; which is the reason why many Veterans are detained in psychiatric wards at local VA hospitals. **How many of these Veterans are detained against their wills, because of statements taken out of context;** which has resulted, in many of these Veterans now having to be heavily sedated on psychotropic medications, which many don't even need!!!

In closing, since when is expressing ones frustration a form of Suicidal Ideation when No Plan or Indent was expressed?

24

Living with PTSD

Living with PTSD and Other Service Connected Injuries Whether Major or Minor

I was not the same when I returned home from deployment, mentally or physically. I no longer knew who I was, but I knew what I'd become; disconnected. I was disconnected from my family, my children, from life. I felt lost and didn't know who, or where to turn; for I'd lost my faith in God and all of what I'd been taught as a little girl, growing up in church and in Sunday school. The foundation from which was built had been crushed from beneath my feet; I felt as though my body was being steadily pulled into an endless hole of no return.

Although many Veterans discovered that picking up from where we left off prior to being deployed was not easy neither was it reality; for many, our reality was that our families, loved-ones and places of employment had gone on without us. Nevertheless, they were not solely to blame, yet many of us were not ready to accept the reality, either. I know I sure wasn't. I couldn't accept that my daughter whom I left at fourteen years old and wearing braces and braids was now sixteen and wearing makeup and dating. I couldn't accept that my son whom was eighteen when I was deployed was now a young man at twenty and in college. I still wanted to be mother, yet I felt that I was robbed of my place and responsibility as being mother, because

I was absent for almost two years of deployment and two years of their lives. I now felt useless, as though I was no longer needed.

I remember prior to being deployed, I would always give my children a kiss and a hug, as well as tell them that I loved them before they went to bed. Thereafter, sometimes during the night I would check in on them, just to watch them sleep; making sure they were breathing well and would cover them with the linen, if they had kicked the linen off. This was something I did, since they were born; until I arrived home from Iraq, all had changed.

If I recall, my son was away at college and my daughter and I had just moved into our new apartment and I was just happy to finally have our own place. Well, it was that night and my daughter was asleep and I walked into her room and I just stood there; looking at her while she was asleep, for I had lost two years of her life. I'd missed this moment of watching her sleep. Nevertheless, in standing over her she sensed my presence and awakened and was startled; which resulted in her screaming and yelling.

At that moment, the loud noise of her yelling and screaming was a trigger for me, because I didn't know what to do; the first instinct that came to mind was to grab her and choke her, because she had startled me with her loud outcry, but I instantly snapped back and caught myself...she was my baby; my daughter; I needed to protect her, so I tried to soothe her, by telling her, "It's me, you're mother". I was in shock; she was in shock; I felt numb; for a moment I'd simply froze. I then realized, something was wrong with me; I wasn't the same; I didn't return the same; I didn't respond the way I would've, had I not been deployed...What happened to me? From that point on, my daughter locked her bedroom door and has never slept with it open or unlocked ever again; even now when she comes home to visit from college, and during the holidays.

After that episode I was hurt, for my little girl was no longer a little girl that I could tuck in at night and watch while she sleeps. She was now sixteen and didn't feel safe sleeping with her bedroom door unlock, just because of her mother, [me] whom did not appear to be the same, prior to being deployed.

Nevertheless, days had gone by and I was having difficulty trying to obtain employment; although I had paid three month advancement on my rent and other bills, I was suffering daily with ongoing excruciating pain from other service-connected injuries that I had also sustained, some while on deployment in Iraq, other injuries were sustained during deployment training in Ft. Hood. Continue visits to the local VA to address my injuries appeared, as though my concerns were falling on deaths ear, I'd lost all faith in God, and my expectation of returning home and picking up from where I left off, was not the same; as a result, I found no use in wanting to stay alive.

Therefore, one night I gave my daughter a kiss goodnight, I locked my bedroom door and I resorted to what was easy, by digesting several number of a particular medication, in an attempt of not awakening.

On the next morning, I was angry. I was angry with myself and once again, I was angry with God. I was angry that all my life I've been subjected to either some form of abuse and trauma, yet I continue to survive through them all. I can't even say I'm a cat of nine lives, because I've lost count as to how many times my life has been spared; but I have no doubt it has been spared more than nine times, for certain. Yes, it may be a good testimonial piece to share, but the experience is something I would never wish on my worst enemy. Yet, I couldn't even take my own life, by simply and intentionally overdosing on some medications.

After I awakened and began remininicing on all of life's abuse and traumas, of which I've been subjected to and all the people lives I've touched in a positive way, that was the moment it came to me, that there may be a reason that my life has been spared, so many times. **Nevertheless, that was the last attempt I've made on my life; and that was in 2005.** Since that ordeal, I've been trying to focus my positive energy on alternative ways of managing my PTSD and my service connected injuries; although I have occasional thoughts when my physical pains become unbearable, but I have no action plan to carry it out.

Moreover, there are many Veterans whom can relate to what was just shared, with regards to wanting to end one's life, due to feeling overwhelmed, helpless, guilt-shamed and/or hopeless; upon returning from deployment. However, having PTSD or any form of a service connected physical injuries, whether major or minor doesn't help matters, especially when the pain is daily, excruciating and ongoing, as well as continuously being advised to take prescription pain medication to mask the symptoms, as though it's a "happy pill" that will make everything better.

The sad part of this is…there are many Veterans whom have been successful in their attempts to take their lives…

The moment of enlightenment for me was when I realize that, there is work for me to do; I am that voice for Veterans and Victims everywhere. Veterans shouldn't have to resort to taking their own lives; because of feeling overwhelmed by a system that is suppose to be available to provide and guide them to receive appropriate services!

25 | Recaps

Veterans, including myself want to be heard; but more importantly, we want to be respected. During my ordeal, with regards to feeling mistreated by my former classmate(s) and professor, I thought I was alone until I later discovered that there were other Veterans whom had been subjected to similar monstrosity of mistreatment on their college campuses.

Although there are some returning Veterans whom may have never experienced being "dismissed without warning"; or may have never received a failing grade, due to a higher priority taking precedent; or may have never been refused an extension to complete a course, due to symptoms from their PTSD being aggravated or triggered; or have ever been berated who dared to disagree, resulting in their grades suffering; these are reported incidents that have actually occurred involving Veterans at various junior and university level colleges across the nation.

As a Veteran, and having to be subjected to the experiences I encountered with some of the students and professor at my university was apparently not an isolated experience. For many of us Veterans whom returned from deployment and who's desire was to further our education, by either utilizing our GI-Bills, Hazelwood Grants or other Vocational Rehabilitative Services; that, was exactly what we wanted to do, without causing any ill feelings or bring any attention to ourselves; neither did we want anyone to see us, nor label us as a victim.

Many of us just wanted to put our experiences behind us; we wanted to move forward, and close that chapter behind us, without having to be reminded of the constant rocket/mortar attacks; being hypervigilant of road side IED's, which we were subjected to on a day to day basis. But more importantly, having to be reminded of the monstrosity of abuse surrounding the sexual assaults, rapes, and ongoing harassments and abuse of power, as well as, racial discriminations is another milestone that many of us too often are reminded of, even within our civilian workplace and environment.

No, surely, that wasn't at all what I wanted to be reminded of, neither was that what any of my Veteran colleagues wanted to be reminded of. Despite, some of the negative remarks that few civilians may want to say about many of us Veterans with PTSD.

Ok, so we may not have returned with a loss of limb or, our loved-ones may not have received the decorative flag for our burial. Does that mean that we're any less disabled? We still have and live with daily mental scars to remind us of our experiences, of which we, too, endured…

Apparently this is a common occurrence that too often is going unaddressed and ignored. Nevertheless, it appears that there is a contradiction with regards to many institutions stating that they promote and support our troops and "patriotism"; yet the actions of many of these students, faculty and professors speaks, otherwise. I wonder? Could the reason that these institutions professing to support Veterans seeking higher education, is it so that they, themselves, can look good to the public or so that they can continue to be federally or state funded? It has to be something; inquiring minds want to know…

Families, friends and loved-ones are our biggest support when we're returning home from deployment; we look to you, as our safe haven from the voices that are forever playing in our heads. You're our escape from the loud noises that we continue to want to block from our ears. You're our shield, when we want to try to isolate from the loud crowds at the local Wal-Mart, and supermarkets; but, all of that and all of your work; as well as all of what you do for us, is in vain, if you begin to judge our length of time [recovery] to when you tell us to **"get over it"**; or when you begin to compare our condition or recovery time to another Veteran who may manage their PTSD symptoms a lot better than ours.

Families, friends and loved-ones have to understand that PTSD is not the same for everyone; thus, every individual progress at their own pace and time, and in their own way; especially given the extent and level of insensitivity of their trauma.

Therefore, the worst thing that a family, friend or a loved-one can do to a Veteran with PTSD, is to judge their length of recovery time and to tell them to **"get over it" or to say, "hasn't it been years since you've been home, shouldn't you've been over that, by now?"** These are wrong statement and questions to convey to any Veteran with PTSD. Statements and a question such as these, will tend to cause a Veteran to feel hopeless, worthless, guilty; most importantly, as though they're untreatable, which often can lead to other internalized thoughts, such as suicidal ideations.

So, family, friends and loved-one aught carefully choose your choice of statements and questions, or say **NOTHING!!!!!!!**

As a Veteran, another interesting inquiry that I'm aware of are available and needed resources and services for other Veterans, when in a crisis situation. I'm also aware that there are other emergency crisis services available within our local community that are not conducive, neither are they equipped to managed the needs or level of care for our returning OIF/OEF Veterans; although many of them believe that they are.

Consequently, the Veteran Crisis Line is the **ONLY** one essential emergency service center that is available to Veterans who are experiencing a mental health crisis. The Veteran Crisis Line has been operational since 2007, and in 2009 added the anonymous online chat service.

Although there are other emergency private agency crisis line service centers within the community willing to assist Veterans, I have found that because of many of their staff **lack** of experience working with the Veteran populations, **lack** of military background and **lack** of Veteran information-resources, too often many Veterans are not provided the high level of services needed, in order to keep them functioning and managing their PTSD.

Moreover, a very interesting factor I've also discovered, is that, too often; especially with few of these emergency mobile/crisis line privately own agencies, many tend to provide a **"one size fit all"** tactic type of approach, when it comes to providing resources, which this tactic may work for the civilian clients, however when it involves Veterans dealing with serious and well intensify trauma from **WAR**, this "one size fit all" tactic is far from being practical…

The type of services Veterans receive at the local Veteran Hospitals, upon returning from deployment can be a lasting impression; whether negative or positive, which includes the Veteran Hospital staff's attitudes, whether courteous and welcoming or rude and unprofessional.

When I returned home from deployment in 2005, there were more negative Veteran reports, re: how long Veterans had to wait in order to receive a post deployment examination, C&P (Compensation & Pension), as well as a mental health appointment; to be assigned an OIF/OEF Psychiatrist/Psychologist/Social Worker, compared to now. I will admit, although the Veteran Healthcare System still have a long way to go, they have improved, somewhat, regarding their turn-around time, in securing prompt appointments to the OIF/OEF returning soldiers, and Veterans population.

Nevertheless, there is always room for improvement…

Because of the first negative impression, of having to wait two - three, sometimes even a month out for a secured first post deployment appointment, this had led to a bad taste in the mouths of many Veterans; resulting in many of them seeking mental health services elsewhere, and outside of the Veteran Healthcare System. Others had taken on another self-care approach, by isolating themselves all together; by banding, and disconnecting all of their affiliation from the Veteran Hospital. This approach is far from being conducive to any returning war Veterans mental state or care of functioning.

This counterproductive approach can lead to a Veteran becoming very unstable, to say the least; easily agitated, irritated, hypervigilant and easily paranoid, due to reliving the traumas from the experiences, which he/she was subjected to while at war in Iraq and/or Afghanistan.

This description of a Veteran is very dangerous to be around, because, not only is he/she a threat to themselves, but now, they're a threat to anyone whom they come in contact with.

Since my return from Iraq it has been very difficult for me to obtain and maintain employment, due to recurrent thoughts of the harassment, which I was repeatedly subjected to, during my entire deployment experience…the constant verbal attacks of being ostracized, berated, taunted and ridiculed; ongoing, by those whom I called in my previous book, "Scarred, but not Broken,"; the Untouchables. Yes, they were just that, Untouchable. The Untouchables, as mentioned in my previous book, "Scarred, but not Broken", were the SFC, the First Sergeant, The Commander, the S-1's and other high Commanding Officers, whom did whatever they wanted to do, to whomever they wanted to do it to, and whenever they wanted to do it too, and no one could say anything.

Well, this is what has continuously been in my thoughts, and has haunted me with every job I've obtained; especially when the supervisors begin to abuse their authority, in the same form and fashion that these untouchables had done. It was without taste, and it was sickening.

Hence, I'm having to live day-by-day and learn how not to slip back into that dark place, but more importantly avoiding narcissistic, asinine supervisors, who also enjoy the fascination of power and control. However, the question is, how do I avoid it? Although, I'm able to come up with only one solution, and that is…to become

Self-Employed; the thought is easier said than done, for some.

Unfortunately, I'm not the only Veteran whom has had difficulty obtaining and maintaining employment; thus there have been other Veterans whom have been quite happy and successful in their endeavors. Yet, others have resorted to becoming their own entrepreneur; for the simple fact that they're not gelling well with either their co-workers or, like me, their supervisors. As a result, entrepreneurship is something many Veterans have opt to become, since they've returned from deployment and have, thus realizing that, working for the civilian sector is a lot difficult than many of us thought it would be; simply because many of these so-called private and non-profit agencies are not willing to invest in taking the time to learn, let alone understand our illness; PTSD...

Yet, they say they want to "Support our Troops; Support our Soldiers; Support our Veterans."

Well, to many of you Private and Non-Profit Agencies, whom have turned away many of us Veterans, who sought employment in your agencies, yet you claim that you want to support us Veterans, with employment; upon our return from deployment; instead of you talking it, let's try walking it. In other words, be Proactive and be part of our added Solutions or Move Over and let another Agency or Organization who will!!!!

26

Where Do I Go From Here?

It has been a long journey for me, since returning from my deployment; I've meant some new acquaintances along the way, as well as lost some along the way. But in the end, I can't say any of them were major lost, because they were just that, acquaintances, not friends. I've heard so often, whether from various pastors while preaching or from actors in movies or plays that, "Some people come into your life for a season; others come into your life for a lifetime." I guess, the secret to it all is, discerning just which one to allow to stay and which one you need to let go. I guess in my case that has never been a problem, because the gift of discernment about people has always been my gift. However, I will admit, my problem many times were, I didn't always want to listen to my gift.

Nevertheless, where do I go from here?

It's been six years since my return from Iraq, and I've accomplished a lot. Nevertheless, within these six years, I've managed to obtain my Master's Degree, as well as became the Author of a very successful book, "Scarred, but not Broken", which is steadily flourishing, since it's been published and released this past April, 2011. "Scarred, but not Broken" was written, on account due to my personal experiences as a single mom, deployed to Iraq.

Moreover, "Scarred, but not Broken" was depicted on the sexual assaults, rapes, harassments and racial discrimination, of which I was subjected to, witnessed, or had knowledge of directly or indirectly. And, although many tend to think of sexual assaults and rape victims as only being just women; well, "Scarred, but not Broken," was not an isolated book that discriminated against or supported any one gender. Hence, it advocated for all victims, men and women. For, this monstrosity of sexual abuse/rapes, as well as racial discrimination is very prevalent and has been ongoing throughout our military branches, for centuries.

Although this is a sensitive topic, that many tend to want to avoid, it must be addressed, for it still appears to be a problem within our Military Branches. Many may be in denial, but racism still exist within our military...Racism is still Alive and Well within "ALL" our Military Branches; yet, when it's time to go to war, we're all fighting the same enemy and we all bleed the same color of blood.. This statement was also made by me on my Facebook.

So, the question is, where do I go from here? I don't know...For, I'm still trying to manage my PTSD on a daily basis; I'm still seeing my regular scheduled Veteran's Therapist; I'm still seeing my regular PCP (Private Care Physician) through the Veteran's Hospital, re: medical care, as well as being monitored and receiving service for my service-connected injuries; whether major or minor and I'm still going through my appeal process. Speaking of appeal process...

Archives of documented reports of Veterans successfully committing suicide, while waiting on decisions made on their appeals, is ludicrous. It should never arrive to this point for any Veteran to succumb to taking their own lives; over not being fairly compensated for either their PTSD illness or a service-connected injury, that causes them day-to day chronic pain. Nevertheless, many of these same Veterans, prior to their demise had been instructed to **"just"** take the medications and "you'll feel better" or that "it will help to alleviate some of your pain"; as though, the medications were a "happy pill"; when, all the long, the medications were simply masking much of their underlying issues, similar to that of a band aide.

With regards to one of my service-connected injuries; let's just say, it has been an ongoing struggle for me to receive any immediate relief. Although my current Veteran Hospital have provided me home therapeutic remedies, to help with some relief; such as, the hot wax paraffin bath and the separate color and texture clay, to help increase strength levels, as well as provided me home aide equipment and devices, to make it convenient for me to not have to reach when taking showers and baths; in addition provided me equipment for other personal hygiene use. These equipment and devices should've been provided to me at the very start of my treatment, upon my return from Iraq, and/or soon after my first post-deployment C & P (Compensation & Pension) Exam.

I'd been wearing a wrist brace since the start of my incident in 2004 (during my deployment); thereafter, I've also been wearing a brace and in chronic pain during every VA exam. It didn't take a rocket scientist to see that I needed some home help aides to assist; such as for daily bathing; toilet business, reaching; picking up; carrying and opening heavy and tight items in and around my home.

Nevertheless, although I'm in pain twenty-four /seven; seven days a week, I try to keep myself and my mind busy, by applying daily activities that I enjoy; one being to advocate for those whom might not otherwise be able to advocate and voice for themselves. However, the only downside of this is, having to type. Although I had been issued an ergonomics keyboard and mouse at my previous place of employment, it still didn't help with prolong use. Typing has been a dilemma for me in the work environment.

Although, I will contest that my previous employer did accommodate me with an ergonomics keyboard and mouse for two months out of the twenty-one months that I was employed with the agency; in order for me to perform my job duties. As for other alternative systems, such as a dictaphone, even if I had a dictaphone for my typing use, I don't believe that it would suffice, for the simple fact that I have a Northern dialect and not a Texan dialect. Therefore, unless the software automatically would be able to decipher the difference in the northern accent; oppose to the southern, with such words as "water" opposed to "whater" or "coffee" opposed to "cuoffee" [laughing], then, I don't see a dictaphone being of much use, either.

So, again; the question is, where do I go from here? (Smile) My response is,

Where there's an Issue that needs to be **Addressed...**

Where there's a Voice that needs to be **Heard...**

Where there's Justice that needs to be **Fair...**

Where there's Equality that needs to be **Reminded...**

Don't be surprised, I may be somewhere close-by, for I am a woman of action; I believe in making the impossible possible.

In closing, I want to give an **Ultimate Thank You** to "**ALL**" whom stood in my way and tried to block my personal-professional-mental growth and intentionally and knowingly tried to cause a trigger for me. I Thank You, for its people like you, who opened the window of opportunity for a Veteran, like me to pursue and advocate for change, as well as bringing awareness within our communities to better service our returning Soldiers, but most importantly, to our transitioning Veterans...

So, I THANK YOU!!!!! For, I've welcomed and I've Prevailed Every Adversity as a Challenge and an Opportunity for Personal – Professional & Mental Growth!!!!!!!

And, although I remain in chronic and ongoing, day to day pain, I'm able to better manage my service connected injury; whether major or minor. By doing this, I'm able to stop and allow my wrist to rest, for that day; followed by soaking it in the hot wax paraffin, and avoiding the habit forming, mind altering pain medications; then, the next day start anew.

I shared that to say this. I'm aware that I have PTSD and other service connected injuries; whether major or minor, nevertheless, I have not allowed my illness or my injuries to hinder me from accomplishing my goals, neither will I allow both to define who I am. For, my illness nor my injuries don't define who I am, neither will I allow both to define who I will become, because who I become is who I choose to become, and not by societies label of PTSD or Service Connected Injury; Whether Major or Minor...

CPSIA information can be obtained
at www.ICGtesting.com
Printed in the USA
FSOW01n1452020315
5473FS